SPEAK
LIKE A
PRO

THE ART AND SCIENCE OF SIGNIFICANT
PUBLIC SPEAKING

BY DAN CLARK, CSP, CPAE

NEW YORK TIMES BEST SELLING AUTHOR
HALL OF FAME SPEAKER
UNIVERSITY PROFESSOR

"You can get anything in life that you want, when you are willing to help enough other people get what they want."

—Zig Ziglar

"Our chief want is someone who will inspire us to be what we know we could become."

—Ralph Waldo Emerson

"Put it before them briefly so they will read it, clearly so they will appreciate it, picturesquely so they will remember it, and accurately so they will be guided by its light."

—Joseph Pulitzer

"The goal in every presentation is to have people leave impressed with themselves, impressed with what they now know that they didn't know before, impressed with what they now can do that they could not do before."

—Bob Pike, Professional Speaker

"The #1 fear of people is not speaking in public. The #1 fear is not speaking well in public. Pressure is not something that is naturally there. It's created when you question your own ability. When you know what you've been trained to do, there is never any question. When you are prepared you never fear. That's why you train and practice so hard – and why this public speaking, presentation skills and communications course is for you!"

—Dan Clark, University Professor

CONTENTS

THE ART OF PUBLIC SPEAKING

THE SCIENCE OF PUBLIC SPEAKING

ACKNOWLEDGMENTS

To Zig Ziglar and Karen and Dr. Jim Koeninger for believing in me in the most significant ways, and literally launching my nationwide career!

To Mrs. Nancy Reagan who invited me into the White House and knighted me as the primary speaker to take her "Just Say No" positive choices program to the schools and teenagers of America.

To my incredible parents – my dad S. Wayne Clark who was an amazing writer and orator, and especially to my sweet, spiritual giant of a woman mother Ruby Maughan Clark who was the one who spawned in me a love for short stories, great jokes, entertaining anecdotes, and deep meaningful metaphors. Because of the influence and positive example of my parents, my sister Debbie and brothers Sam and Paul, I am a Hall of Fame professional speaker!

For my special teachers who believed in me when others wouldn't: Ms. Dubois, Mrs. Inman, Dr. Morray, Mrs. Smart, Principal Richards, Mr. Croft, Mr. Thorem and Coaches Gene Thompson, Din Morris, Brooks, Allen, Wageman, Trost, Martin, Weight, Simons, Banker, Zimmer, McBride, and Gadd.

For Russ Anderson, Elder Craig Zwick, Don Pugh, Doug Miller, Fran Peak, Dick Nourse, Norm Gibbons, Lila Bjorkland, Micky Fisher, Jennifer Lapine, Ernie Wilhoit, Don Wilson, Kay Baker, Pat Mutch, Steve Cosgrove, Les Hewitt, Don Gale, Michael Gale, Chuck Coonradt, Charles Reid, Steve Munn, Paul Clark, Kelly Clark, Gen. Hal Hornburg (Ret.), Maj. Gen. Johnny Weida, and Laura Calchera (Supreme Commander) for helping me launch my career and/or take it to the next level.

For my National Speakers Association inspiration: Mark Victor Hansen, Jack Canfield, Gail Larsen, Naomi Rhode, Dave Gordon, Robert Henry, Renee Strom, Keith Harrell, Roger Crawford, Bubba Bechtol, Grady Jim Robinson, Jim Tunney, Jeanne Robertson, Bob

Murphy, Patricia Fripp, Ray Pelletier, Max Dixon, Mark Sanborn, Chad Hymas, Jason Hewlett, Devin Thorpe, Rob Waldman and Art Berg.

For Bill Kimball, Bob and Paul Mendenhall, Dick Clissold, Bill Gibbs, Jay Jensen, Bob Raybould, Lincoln Hanks, Pres. Royden and Sister Derrick, Phillip Gibson, Mark Tuttle, Gary Mangum, Scott Buie, Mark Monsen, Mont Beardall, Blain Hope, Todd Petersen, Colin and Theresa Dunne, Brendan and Evelyn Gibney, Todd Morgan, Brad Morris, Brent Bowen, Walt and Peggy Plumb, David Spafford, Todd Larsen, Todd Cook, Jason Bourne and David Ayre for your spirituality, commitment to obedience, faith, and influence in my Christian walk with God.

For K.C., Danny, Nikola, McCall, and Alexandrea for finding wisdom, comfort, laughter, and solace in my speeches, stories, anecdotes, and words. I love you and need you in my life forever.

ZIG ZIGLAR RECOMMENDATION

Who for 30 years personally mentored Dan in The Art of Motivational Teaching, The Science of Storytelling, The Mechanics of Platform Presentation Skills, and The Privilege of the Platform

"Let me introduce and endorse my friend, Dan Clark. I met him in 1982, and sponsored him into the National Speakers Association, where in 1987 he became one of the youngest ever to earn his CSP – Certified Speaking Professional designation in the history of NSA. In the last 30 years, Dan has spoken an average of over 150 times a year to millions of people all over the world. The neat thing is he gets repeat engagements. That really says something about the man. Interestingly enough, his versatility has taken him into some of the outstanding comedy clubs in America where he entertains and speaks. Dan is also a musician with considerable talent, having written a number of songs for some of the great talent in Nashville.

When you look at all of the things Dan Clark has done, you've got to be impressed. When you look at the man, you've got to be impressed. In fact, he will go down as one of the outstanding salespeople of all time. In my judgment, maybe the greatest I've ever seen.

With all of this, Dan is a marvelous human being, one who practices what he preaches, one who has his life in balance, one whose family is extraordinarily important to him, and one who is committed to bringing a message of hope and encouragement to any kind of audience he speaks to and/or for. Dan is one of the truly outstanding speakers in our world with a lot of good information that he delivers in an inspirational and humorous manner. He speaks and writes from his head and heart to your head and heart.

Most importantly, he's a man of integrity. It's more than a cliché to say that what you see is what you get in Dan Clark. I encourage you to invite him to speak to your group. You'll be glad that you did."

—World Renown Motivational Teacher Zig Ziglar

"I am a fan of Dan Clark. Every time we've shared the stage together, it is his devotion to service and unwavering belief in the value of putting others before ourselves, that attracts me to his message."

—Simon Sinek
TED Speaker/Best Selling Author 'Start With Why'

"Thanks Dan. Our time together has enabled me to really make a breakthrough. Your words have been life changing and your approach enabled me to understand the technical and spiritual side of public speaking."

—Kareem Abdul-Jabbar
NBA Hall of Famer

"My man Dan Clark is a friend, mentor and the heavyweight champion of the world when it comes to how to write and deliver a speech. Not only has Dan helped me get in touch with who I really am and in tune with my message and why I want to share it with the world, but through the principles, techniques and insights taught in this book, Dan has helped me transition from professional entertainment athlete to professional speaker.

I recommend this book and Dan's public speaking program to every celebrity who has achieved success. No longer is it acceptable for athletes to come across as 'dumb jocks.' One's speaking ability should match one's performance ability in sports, film and music. Dan Clark is the guru and, until he can fit you into his schedule, this book can be your trainer."

—Diamond Dallas Page
3 Time World Champion WWE Professional Wrestler

FOREWORD

Since 1982, I have been a full-time professional speaker. In contrast with my three siblings—who own a large insurance agency, successfully sell real estate, and manage a prestigious investment banking firm—when my mother is asked what I do, she answers, "Dan? Oh, he talks. We're so proud." Speaking for a living is a curious profession, and one that has been very good to me. Not only has it taken me all over the world and allowed me to share the platform with some of the most powerful, interesting, and famous people on our planet, but it has also given me the opportunity to positively touch people's lives and change the world one story at a time. My mom proudly brags that I am "the best speech she ever delivered!"

If you are an emerging leader, seasoned corporate executive, military officer/NCO, coach or educator, it is critical to your leadership effectiveness and opportunities for organizational promotion that you remain aware of seven fundamental truths:

1. In sports, music, and drama, even the very best professional athletes, singers, and actors in the world have coaches/teachers/directors who require and inspire them to learn the plays and material, and perfectly practice, until it becomes a subconscious mental and muscle memory they can automatically execute in every performance. Shouldn't you also have an executive coach in the art of public speaking and the science of presentation/sales skills who teaches and mentors you to become and remain a world-class influencer?

2. We all know managers have power and authority that is appointed, with subordinates whom they boss around, while working as subordinates who are bossed around. Leaders have influence and respect that is earned, and have followers, which

is a voluntary decision to let the leader inspire and guide them because they are charismatic communicators.

3. We also know that the number one qualifying requirement for being a leader is one's ability to articulately speak in a sophisticated, elegant, polished professional way that teaches and inspires others to make your priorities their priorities.

4. There is no justification for the cost of gathering people together in a meeting and paying a speaker's honorarium on an academic basis only. If the program is strictly educational and on PowerPoint, just email the content slides to everyone and let them study it on their own dime, at their own pace. We are emotional relational beings. Emails, texts, and PowerPoint presentations are mere rational exchanges of information, which usually dilute the very purpose of up-close and personal interaction and should seldom be part of a heart-to-heart discussion and spirit-to-spirit exchange of energy, personality, purpose, and plan. Remember, reason leads to conclusions, but it is emotion that leads to action!

5. The purpose of every meeting and the mission of every presenter should be to clarify 'why' the organization exists, re-energize individual motivation, build character, set higher expectations, provide training that not only improves skill but develops loyalty, engagement, attitude, duty, excellence in all you do, respect, service before self, honor, integrity, and personal courage, so the attendees depart as stronger men and women committed to make winning personal as they relentlessly strive to be stalwarts in the organization and in their communities.

6. This course is for those who feel "called" to share their own stories and material as a corporate executive, entrepreneur, military leader, manager, coach, educator, or sales champion

with the polish of a "professional speaker" who can trigger passion, creativity, imagination, and greater resolve in the hearts and minds of their subordinates/audience members/ listener(s), give them an unforgettable emotional experience they can't get at home and work, and take them to an intellectual and emotional place they cannot take themselves!

7. For these reasons, whenever we are given the opportunity and responsibility to present to a single individual or to a large group, it is critical that we realize the responsibility of the Privilege of the Platform.

In the attitude of "giving back," and because so many people are like the tiny child standing on his tiptoes, craning his neck to peer up on the table and see what all the colorful things are, I have penned this comprehensive guide on the art and science of speaking in public. The following chapters include twelve of the most frequently asked questions about public speaking, along with my answers, and will allow me to teach everything I know about presentations, preparation, interviewing, crafting a speech, facilitating small group interactive training, and keynoting to a huge group on a big stage with large-room platform skills.

So that you won't have to pass through the same tight spaces that I did to become a good communicator, and because I am buoyed up by the thought that in my 35 plus years as a professional speaker, I have actually acquired some knowledge and experience that is worth sharing on this subject. Because there might be someone—you—out there who will enter into this magnificent profession as a result of my sharing, I present this book.

MUST-READ INTRODUCTION

When I was in college, one professor required that we read *Oedipus Rex* by Sophocles. The most memorable, yet twisted part of the play for me is when Oedipus unknowingly does some terrible things, and when he realizes it, he feels that the only way he can make amends is to be punished. Consequently, he blinds himself. The thought that someone would deliberately blind himself not only troubled me when I read it, but it has remained a source of internal excavation ever since, especially now that I am a professional speaker.

Having a job that encompasses teaching, inspiring, influencing, guiding, and taking people's hearts to places their minds can never go has not only made me more aware of how many misguided, short-sighted, and blatantly "blind" people there are among us, but it has re-introduced me to a familiar quote, rekindled a curiosity to deepen my understanding of it, and recommit to never letting it happen to me.

"When the blind lead the blind, they both fall into the ditch," refers to mental, emotional, topical, moral, ethical, and spiritual blindness. At first glance, the focus of this truism seems to be about the perils that come to a follower who has been blinded by the craftiness of a blind, charismatic leader. In a larger corporate, association, church, or school sense, behavioral anthropologists call this blindness "social proof," where we are emotionally moved to follow the crowd because there is strength in numbers and everybody else is following the ever-growing crowd.

In the context of this book, I want to focus on the other side of the "blind leading the blind" involving those in the lead whose mission it is to help their blind followers and listeners to see. When a manager, educator, preacher, or speaker is blind, they cannot fulfill this responsibility. It's only a matter of time before they find themselves and their people in the "ditches" of life. Of course, some claim their blindness is because they had a blind leader perpetuate what their blind leader perpetuated, and they don't know any better than to also pass this blindness along. But we all know this is the exception, not the rule.

Most blind leaders suffer from the same self-inflicted blindness evidenced in our own lives when we refuse to see the danger or evil in our choice of beliefs, friends, business interests, influences, health habits, and environments. Each of us could avoid the pain that inevitably results from such self-deception if we would simply let go of traditions based on who is right and start developing convictions based on what is right. Bad eyesight can always be corrected with good insight.

I often see this self-inflicted "Oedipus blindness" in the world of professional speaking. The unwritten expectation of the National Speakers Association is that all members will become "polished," and as one who respects and fully supports NSA, I have relentlessly pursued this classification for nearly three decades. Where the blindness occurs is in the misinterpretation of what "polished" means. I have seen too many so-called polished speakers bomb in their speeches. Why? How can this happen?

Some of the biggest wigs in professional speaking have turned a blind eye to the true definition of "polished" and have perpetuated it. If polished means a completely memorized speech with choreographed movements, practiced punctuated pauses, forced gestures, imitated voice inflections, and no desire for spontaneity, then being polished only makes you an accomplished actor starring in your own play. Sure, they loved you in Chicago on Thursday, but you didn't connect with your Orlando audience on Saturday. Is it their fault?

No! You have been blinded by a motivation to make a speech rather than to make a difference. These are the speakers referred to as "slick" who give the profession a bad name; the "soothsayers" who say soothing things the same smooth way every single time. These are not the extraordinary speakers. They are merely polished presenters.

However, if "polished" means "Significant" because you have taken the time to think through what you believe, why you believe it, and what you know that will help others succeed, you realize that your words of wisdom are not a hypocritical hoax, but rather a natural exposure of your passion for living that is the real you offstage.

For this reason, being a "significant speaker" is not showing up and presenting "speech A" so the audience is impressed with you. But rather being present in the moment, dedicated to carrying on an "inspirational conversation" with a continual transformational "polishing" that occurs during your speech where you move from *hyper* entertainer, to *helper* with their needs, to *healer* of their pain, to *host* of their new possibilities.

Of course, there is an art to "Significant" public speaking and a science to preparing a speech, but both success and failure boil down to only one question: What kind of communicator do you want to be? Will you open your eyes and free your personality to be the speaker you have the capacity to be? Or like Oedipus, will you self-inflict a blindness that holds you hostage to the mechanical role of doing what mere presenters do? By the end of this book you will SEE what I mean!

THE ART OF
PUBLIC
SPEAKING

THE PRIVILEGE OF THE PLATFORM

Privilege of the Platform, is a phrase that was coined and created by a former president of the National Speakers Association, the sophisticated, elegant, polished, and professional Naomi Rhode. Naomi is one of those charismatic individuals spoken of who has influenced her industry forever as a role model for every speaker who knows her. In her year as president of NSA, Naomi chose for her tenured theme "The Privilege of the Platform." It epitomizes the significant responsibility each one of us has whenever we are allowed to speak in public. It had a powerful effect on me then and still does to this day as it serves as a constant reminder to never take for granted any opportunity to touch someone's life. Because she has influenced so many, I am inspired to also do my part in whatever way I can.

CHAPTER ONE

WHY EVERYBODY SHOULD BECOME AN EXTRAORDINARY COMMUNICATOR

In Proverbs 16:23 King Solomon reminds us: "The heart of the wise makes his speech judicious, and adds persuasiveness to his lips." To me, this suggests that when you figure out what you believe, and become so convicted in that belief that you feel compelled and morally obligated to share the practical application wisdom of what you know with the world, you can and will become an extraordinary communicator!

When I was in high school I was so skinny I had to jump around in the shower to get wet! I could no more stand in front of a room and give a speech than recite the Chinese alphabet backwards! And no, you don't have to have some exotic fantastic story where you got in an accident and your head was cut off, but you still speak fluent French! Guaranteed, people will listen to you when you have something meaningful to say – and can deliver it in a polished, articulate, entertaining, compelling, professional way!

Steve Jobs said, "The most powerful person in the world is the storyteller. The storyteller sets the vision, values and agenda of an entire generation that is to come."

Dale Carnegie said: "85% of our financial success is due to our personality and ability to communicate. Shockingly, only 15% is due to knowledge and technical skill."

While speaking to business students at Columbia University in 2009, billionaire Warren Buffet said, "Mastering the art of public speaking is the single greatest skill to boost your career. Once you improve it – will raise your personal value by 50%."

TED Talk curator Chris Anderson said, "As a leader – as an entrepreneur – as an advocate influencer – public speaking is the key to unlocking empathy, stirring excitement, sharing knowledge and insights, and promoting a shared dream."

And my colleague Jarod Kintz observed, "99% of the population is afraid of public speaking and of the remaining 1%, 99% of them have nothing original and interesting to say."

"Our national survey revealed that 63% of employees in America would rather receive a promotion than a raise in pay, 38% expected to be promoted after spending two years in a role, and that the fastest way to climb the corporate ladder is by becoming an extraordinary communicator and expert presenter."

—Korn Ferry

As one who has been a full-time professional speaker for over 35 years, I agree! In fact, research shows that our success or failure in business, marriage, and parenting is determined by our ability to communicate! Obviously, you have purchased this book and are studying the art and science of public speaking for your own reason. But there are eight universal reasons we all can agree on that will make mastering the art of speaking in public extremely important in your life:

1. At some point in your life you will need to deliver a powerful and memorable speech, so you might as well get good at it before the call comes.

2. You will increase in self-confidence, which makes you more comfortable around other people.

3. The unique skills learned will boost performance in other areas of life, where you are given more responsibility at work, generate more sales, and/or land a better job.

4. Becoming a significant communicator will generate a higher level of respect and admiration from everybody in your life.

5. It gives you a reason to improve upon your knowledge, because one of the best ways to learn is to teach.

6. It differentiates you in the workforce because it allows you to demonstrate your knowledge.

7. If you want to be a leader, you must become an articulate, polished, public speaker, which is the most effective way to form a tribe of supporters around you, knowing leadership is earned, having little to do with a title or authority.

8. Life is a story – and family history is passed from generation to generation through stories – and you have some incredible experiences worth sharing – and everybody loves to hear a great story – so you owe it to yourself to become a master storyteller and experience the inspirational impact of a well told tale!

CHAPTER TWO

DOES PUBLIC SPEAKING MAKE YOU NERVOUS?

Experts remind us, "If we are prepared, we shall not fear." Fear has been defined as False Evidence Appearing Real. I agree. So it baffles me that experts also tell us that people's number one fear is speaking in public. Ahead of death, spiders, snakes, and the rest of the top ten, standing up in front of people and delivering a speech is the scariest thing we can do? I don't think so.

My greatest fear is the fear of failing—but "proper prior planning and perfect practice prevent poor performance." Preparing ourselves to speak and then preparing the speech eliminates fear. We have gone full circle. Getting nervous is described as "getting butterflies." Preparation gets our butterflies to fly in formation. Nervous energy properly directed is an adrenaline shot that brings us to life on stage.

Being nervous keeps us from ever becoming complacent and taking our speaking responsibility lightly. Being nervous before any big event is good, not bad, and in reality is really nothing more than anticipation, excitement, and internal validation that we are finally ready to test our preparation and display our practiced execution.

I've been there. There is nothing more exhilarating than standing on the five-yard line in a huge football stadium packed full of sixty thousand screaming fans, waiting for the opening kickoff with nervous energy, focusing on what I'm going to do with the ball when it is kicked to me!

I experience this same feeling every time the emcee of a meeting begins introducing me to speak. For me, taking the stage and grabbing the microphone is catching the kickoff, running with the ball, and by the end of my speech, scoring a touchdown to win the game!

One humorous experience puts into perspective the perils of perception: I flew into Dallas, Texas, to speak at the convention center. I spent the night at the Hyatt Hotel at the DFW airport. It had been arranged that the husband of the meeting planner would pick me up the next morning and take me downtown for my speech. That night the hotel restaurant had an all-you-can-eat seafood buffet. I must have eaten at least fifty shrimp and clams before turning in.

In the middle of the night I woke up with food poisoning. Now, I'm not talking a few stomach cramps here. I'm telling you, I was having labor pains! It felt like somebody had kicked me in the groin and then grabbed my bottom lip and pulled it up over my head! Not only did I throw up all the seafood, but I swear I popped out some Hot Tamales and Red Vines I had eaten in the ninth grade!

With no sleep, my wake-up call alerted me to shave, shower, and put on my suit and tie. I wandered through the restaurant on my way to the lobby, downed two pieces of toast and a handful of soda crackers (trying to settle my stomach), and walked outside to greet my ride. He was in his airline captain's uniform, standing at attention, and in a military, matter-of-fact voice asked, "Are you Mr. Clark?" I acknowledged, got in his car, and we proceeded on our way.

DFW airport is one of the largest airports in the United States and it takes thirty minutes just to get off the premises. Within five minutes of beginning our drive, I quietly asked, "Could you please pull over?" The captain had not said one word to me up to this point, and because I was so weak, I hadn't pushed for conversation either. He said, "What? Right here?"

Fighting back a dry heave I blurted, "Yes, now." He slowly put on his blinker and pulled over. I opened the door and totally lost it: "Ralph! Joy! Wha, yaa, ha!" I wiped my mouth clean, closed the car door, and sat up straight. He drove on. Ten minutes later, still without a word from the captain, I burped, "Can you stop again?" This time he jerked the wheel to the right and in a 3-g turn he pulled over and slammed on the brakes.

Again, I opened the door, hung out of the car, and called for Ralph and Joy again. When I shut the door, he had both hands on the wheel and was sternly staring straight ahead. He sped the rest of the way to the airport exit.

We finally arrived at the convention center but couldn't find a parking spot close to the front entrance. I don't know why the captain didn't just drop me off. Maybe he thought he shouldn't leave me alone, or maybe he thought he should talk to his wife before she met me. In any case, we parked forever away and started to walk. At one hundred degrees with 90 percent humidity and me sporting a dark suit and tie, it only took a few seconds for me to hang a left and sprint to a fence where I could pop my cookies without hitting a car.

Wiping my chin for the third time, I rejoined my escort for the grand entrance into the convention center. As we got to the door, the stoic captain finally broke his silence. "Mr. Clark, may I ask you a personal question?"

I whispered, "Yes."

He asked, "Do you always get this nervous before you speak?"

CHAPTER THREE

SO... YOU WANT TO BE A PUBLIC SPEAKER?

Then you must understand there are two primary teaching pedagogies:

1. "Discovery Learning," where the speaker/instructor asks a question and the listeners/students use their personal experiences and resources to answer the question and solve the problem.

2. "Direct and Explicit Instruction," where the speaker/instructor takes the listeners/students through a four-step process:
    - I Do.
    - We Do.
    - You All Do It Together With Partners As A Group.
    - You Do It As An Individual.

The Art of Significant Public Speaking and Storytelling constitutes a combination of both teaching models by creating meaning with your listeners through the transference of trust, knowledge, and wisdom in a thought-provoking, emotionally-stimulating, unforgettable way.

Because the definition of wisdom is 'applied knowledge' we never learn just to know. We learn to do. The art of public speaking is about doing everything in our power to connect at the right brain, relational, touchy, feely, emotional side with a focus on the 'spirit of the laws' of communication. Obviously, there is a difference between teaching and talking. Obviously, there is a difference between leadership, power and authority, which means you can be a leader without a title.

If something is important to you, you will always find a way – when it's not, you will always find an excuse. When you know what you firmly believe and have a passionate personal reason to share it, overcoming your fear of speaking in public subsides through preparation – especially when you spend more time preparing yourself to speak than you spend preparing a speech.

The Science of Significant Public Speaking and Storytelling is a focus on the 'letter of the laws' of communication divided into the seven templates we use in preparing our speeches. As we follow these preparation formulas we actually mitigate our so-called fear realizing F.E.A.R. does not mean: Forget Everything And Run. F.E.A.R. means: False Evidence Appearing Real, so you Face Everything And Rise.

The four primary purposes of public speaking are to entertain, to persuade, to inform or to teach. Therefore, in the course of your life you will definitely be asked to deliver a powerful, memorable speech in one of these seven categories:

SEVEN SPEECH CATEGORIES

1. **Entertaining Speech**: Usually a luncheon or after dinner speech with a light message, lots of laughs, under 30 minutes long!

2. **Impromptu Speech**: Although you may not recognize it as such, we engage more in impromptu speeches on a daily basis than any other form of public speaking. No, they are not "off-the-cuff" as most believe, but rather, "spur-of-the moment" opportunities to express ourselves in an organized delivery using the "Eight Elements of Organizing a Speech." Most of the time when you are called upon to deliver an Impromptu Speech you will be given a few minutes to gather and structure your thoughts before you speak.

3. **Extemporaneous Speech**: Either persuasive or informative in nature, with little or no advance preparation, which validates that you should spend less time preparing a speech and more time preparing yourself to speak.

4. **Persuasive Speech**: Every speech should be a smooth, dynamic performance that has an introduction that catches the listener's attention, a clearly stated thesis or theme of the speech, formatted in a structure that provides social proof, incorporates research, background knowledge, and opinion, followed by a conclusion, which summarizes the speech. A persuasive speech specifically focuses on your ability to craft a coherent argument about a topic that is both relevant and interesting in your life, which makes us believe and agree with you so we engage in your cause. (Explained in great detail later in the book.)

5. **Informative Speech**: Focused on your ability to teach and inform your listener(s) about a topic both interesting and relevant in their lives. This means you will be an authority on the topic you are presenting, which is never trivial or of common knowledge to the class. Stretch yourself. Teach us something significant!

    An "Informative Speech" is a fact-based speech intended to teach its audience about a specific topic. Informative speeches must have thesis statements and reliable sources for each claim. Some presenters opt to use slides, photographs or other visual aids to enhance their informative speeches.

    An informative speech may focus on general information, such as the history of motorcycles, or applicable information, such as teaching the audience how to overhaul a carburetor. Unlike a persuasive speech where the speaker includes his conclusions and opinions alongside the sourceable facts, an informative speech provides just the facts and allows the audience to draw their own conclusions.

The topic options for informative speeches are nearly limitless and are not limited to non-fiction ideas. For example, it would be possible to write an informative speech about the Harry Potter universe by using quotations from the books, excerpts from interviews with the author and sales figures from the publishing company.

Controversial Informative Speech: Before speaking about a controversial topic, make sure you acquire a thorough knowledge of both sides of the topic and understand the general opinion or bias of the audience, remaining tactful and objective, and most respectful of your opportunity to share. Obviously, the topic is oftentimes very close to the speaker's heart, making it difficult to remain objective. And knowing that controversial topics can produce angry responses from some listeners, it is critically important to be confident in yourposition and not to exaggerate the truth.

6. **Instructive Speech**: Focused only on teaching a specific skill set knowledge in a sequential, non-variable, step-by-step methodical way. 3-D diagrams, graphs and charts are definitely utilized with an emphasis on the "Direct Instruction" teaching pedagogy to accentuate a hands-on experience. An Instructive Speech is always a Training Speech followed by both a written and a practicum exam with a graduation certification awarded at completion. While information, knowledge, wisdom, talent, character, class, work ethic and love are transferable from relationship to relationship, job to job, and location to location (no matter where you go, there you are!) an Instructive Training Speech teaches a specific skill set (i.e. repairing jet engines, hitting a 90 mph fastball, performing a heart transplant) that is not transferable from relationship, job and location to a

different relationship, job and location, specific only to the required task and current responsibility at hand.

7. **The Three Special Occasion Speeches:** A Tribute to someone special, a Toast to a leader, coworker, and/or friend at a birthday party, wedding or social gathering, and a Eulogy about someone who has died.

TRIBUTE

A Tribute is a 'commemorative' speech with the single purpose of inspiring, celebrating and uniting listeners in sincere, heartfelt gratitudeand admiration for its subject. The occasions that call for a tribute speech include: Anniversaries, Reunions, Awards Ceremonies, Retirements, and Weddings (although the 'Best Man' and 'Father-of-the-Bride' speeches at weddings are often called Toasts, because of their content and intent they are actually Tribute Speeches).

Whether the focus is a person or a group of people, the characteristics of a Tribute Speech are admiration and respect with a focus on their positive qualities, highlighting accomplishments by reflecting on the contribution of the group or person on the lives of others.

A Tribute (an extraordinary accomplishment, a significant life well lived) is one of the greatest gifts you can give to a friend/colleague.

THE FOUR ELEMENTS OF WRITING AND DELIVERING A POWERFUL, MEMORABLE TRIBUTE

1. **Brainstorm the Many Possibilities to Write About**
   - Consider your audience as well as the person you're writing about

- How you knew this person personally
- The person's characteristics
- The person's accomplishments
- A special side of this person
- The person's lasting impact
- A funny or touching memory that was not shared widely
- Writing a Tribute Speech for your mother will be very different than writing one for a friend.

2. **Outline**

   When writing a Tribute remember it is an actual speech. Itis not an Extemporaneous, Impromptu, Persuasive, or short humorous Toast. It is an Informational Speech that must havea catchy beginning, powerful content and an emotional close.For this reason, you should organize your thoughts and stories and write an Outline – printed on 3X5 cards for your reference while speaking:

   - Introduction
   - Main Point 1
   - Evidence
   - Main Point 2
   - Evidence 2
   - Conclusion

3. **Finish Strong**

   Conclude on an emotional note. A quote or poem is a wonderful way to consolidate your remarks. You could ask the audience to remember their own favorite memory of this person or to think of them when they visit a certain place. * Usually a 5 to 10 Minute Speech.

4. **Practice**

- Think of your speech as a performance, not just a reading
- Make eye contact with your audience
- Stand up straight and tall
- Focus on your storytelling skills
- Let your passion show

TOAST

Giving a strong toast involves much more than simply standing up and saying whatever pleasantries come to mind. The perfect toast is short, funny, heart felt, is about three minutes long, and follows a specific structure that requires practice.

When the time comes to speak, begin by standing up and simply raising your glass toward the center of your room to indicate that you are about to begin. Because it is an honor to give a toast, and realize that the toast is not about you, the contents should include a brief background on how you are connected to the person you are toasting, a story that does not embarrass anyone or make guests uncomfortable, a hook and a catchy conclusion.

A Toast (wedding, gala, awards banquet) is one of the greatest gifts you can give to a friend/colleague.

THE SEVEN ELEMENTS OF WRITING AND DELIVERING AN UNFORGETTABLE TOAST

1. **Identify Yourself**. There will be people who don't know who you are. Take no more than 30 seconds to briefly introduce yourself and explain your relationship to the person(s). When it's a wedding, the Hosts, Maid of Honor, Best Man and Newlyweds themselves (in this order) are traditionally the ones to take the mic.

2. **Thank the Hosts**. When you begin, acknowledge the ones who have invited all of you there and are paying for the event. Being grateful and gracious shows you're being thoughtful so that when you become 'grandiose,' the audience is ready and willing to accept what you say next.

3. **Focus on only One Inspiring Topic**. Loyal friendship, adventure, character (trustworthy, disciplined, resilient, service, unconditional love).

4. **Share Supporting Memories**. Your value as a toast-maker is your first-hand personal experiences with the individuals(s). In doing this, you're giving the attendees an inside view of that person, or couple, that they've probably never known before. * If you're going to use humor, make sure it's classy, not vulgar, racist, sexist, political or blatantly religious. Be sure to balance your humor with emotional undercurrents to provide depth.

5. **Summarize**. Clarify how everything you just mentioned led up to the current moment and how the person you are toasting is a better, happier, more complete and fulfilled human being because of the person (spouse) sitting next to him/her or because of the significant individual influencers in the room.

6. **Congratulate**. Make sure to applaud the union of the couple or the significance of the award and recognition he/she is receiving. This is the whole reason why you're here!

7. **End with an Invitation**. "Please charge your glasses and join me in a Toast to (say both names) that they may always be there for each other, as they have been there for each of us – that they will always remember: happily-ever-after is a day-at-a-time proposition. Cheers to your amazing future!" Or…

- Practice your Toast so you Don't Read It! List the Seven Elements in outline form on a 3X5 card (it's thick and won't shake if you get nervous). Print the Keyword or Quote/Phrase in each of the Seven Elements that will trigger your Point/Story to keep you organized and on task.

- Time it. Toasts should be no longer than 3 minutes (maximum 5 mins) long enough time to share a sweet/fun memory and sentiment so guests don't lose interest.

- Keep Drinks to a Minimum. If you are a drinker and giving a toast, stick to one glass of 'bubbly'. Too much alcohol can turn your carefully crafted sentiments into a big, slurred mess that could literally ruin the entire occasion.

- Examples of a Humorous and Heartfelt Toast:

"Mark and I were roommates in college and were your stereotypical wild and undisciplined freshman looking for ourselves! So, when Mark read that drinking was bad for you, he stopped reading! Ha! In fact, Mark drank so much that when he dies, if we cremate his body, we will never get the flame to go out! Haha! So, let us Toast his beloved Sarah who loved him off the 'Highway To Hell' and onto the 'Stairway To Heaven'" to being the extraordinary human being that he is! Cheers to their continuous journey together as they encourage each other to be the best versions of themselves!"

"We all know how John and Julie's third date was sort a train wreck between his dog ripping her dress and the food poisoning from the dinner he cooked. But I don't think any of us, including John, has ever heard Julie describe it that way. Because she already knew that John was the one whether he liked it or not. Thankfully, John came around and has

34

definitely 'out-kicked his coverage!' Yes, they came from completely different backgrounds with an unlikely union, and so I say Cheers to Julie and John who show us why and how the road between the impossible and the possible is forever paved."

EULOGY

Eulogies should not be confused with obituaries, which are published biographies recounting the lives of those who have recently died. A Eulogy is a speech or writing in praise of a person or thing who has died, usually given as part of a memorial funeral service when the religious tradition allows it. Its primary purpose is to provide comfort or inspiration, as well as establishing a connection to the person whom the Eulogy is in behalf of. For example:

President Reagan's eulogy for the Challenger space shuttle crew (1986):

"I know it is hard to understand, but sometimes painful things like this happen. It's all part of the process of exploration and discovery. It's all part of taking a chance and expanding man's horizons. The future doesn't belong to the fainthearted; it belongs to the brave. The Challenger crew was pulling us into the future, and we'll continue to follow them."

Charles Spencer's eulogy for Princess Diana (1997):

"Diana was the very essence of compassion, of duty, of style, of beauty. All over the world she was a symbol of selfless humanity, a standard-bearer for the rights of the truly downtrodden, a truly British girl who transcended nationality, someone with a natural nobility who was classless, who proved she needed no royal title to continue to do good!"

CHAPTER FOUR

ARE THERE COMMUNICATION SYSTEMS AND FORMULAS?

KNOWLEDGE + MOTIVATION = PEAK PERFORMANCE

Let me briefly take you into my world and explain this in terms of writing and speaking. Readers and audiences don't care what I've done. They care what I've learned. Even more, they care what they will learn from me. The goal of any book or seminar should be to help others turn success into significance. This is a double-edged sword. First, the author or speaker must prepare and see himself not as a Training Provider but as a Training Adviser. If he is merely writing or presenting, the reader or seminar attendee only becomes impressed with the author or speaker. However, if the book or seminar truly trains and advises, the reader or attendee becomes impressed with himself and closes the book or leaves the seminar as his own motivator. Providers are short-term, opinionated, and accepted. Advisers are long-term, factual, and trusted.

Some leaders or organizations see training as an interruption and cost. Do you? Organizations that are truly in the people-building business, that actually want to win with desired results, have leaders who look at training as an investment. And the Return on Investment (ROI)? Both management and labor become the change they wish to see, and when held accountable, give results not reasons. They realize there is no failure, only feedback. Because the investment was not in "providers" but in "advisers," the long-term ROI is that everybody in the organization, from the top down and side to side, is committed to execute the following formula on their own and keep the book or seminar relevant and active in both their personal and professional lives.

This formula was developed by my friend and colleague, Mr. Bob Pike. I recommend him as one of the premier trainers of trainers, trusted advisers, and success coaches on the planet. He is based out of Minneapolis and can be reached at BobPikeCTT@aol.com. Bob simplifies and quantifies the necessity to blend facts and inspired feelings. I respectfully refer to this simple, profound equation as Pike's Peak Performance Process.

$$K + M = P\,P$$
(Knowledge plus Motivation equals Peak Performance)

$$K - M = L\,E\,I$$
(Knowledge minus Motivation equals Less than Expected Improvement)

$$M - K = EI$$
(Motivation minus Knowledge equals Energized Incompetence)

Notice that Knowledge *minus* Motivation *disappoints* and Motivation *minus* Knowledge breeds *Mediocrity*. As Mr. Miyagi counseled in the movie *Karate Kid*, "Ambition without knowledge is like a boat on dry land." To succeed at anything, and then to take that success to the highest performance level called significance, requires an equal measure of Motivation and Knowledge. One without the other is a waste. I see this truth in certain religions in the world that suggest a once-a-month fast. But fasting without purpose and prayer is just going without food!

I also see this in the speaking profession. Some speakers eloquently "heat up" the audience and give them a rah-rah "sunburn" that is bright red for a few days with excitement, sensitivity, and revitalized resolve. And yes, after a few more days the "burn" fades into a "tan" where they are feeling better and optimistic that they can sustain the new healthy look. But it's only a matter of time before they start to "peel" and the momentary new tan-colored outside reverts back to the old pale "real" beneath it all. As they say, "Motivation without education is frustration – we need a blend of facts and feelings. We always need high touch in a high tech world!"

ABOVE ALL RELATE!

There is also a communications formula for relating to every audience based on a true principle that I will refer to again and again: "The only place from which people can grow is where they are. To be a "significant speaker" we must go where our audience members are physically, intellectually and emotionally. Only there can we gently invite them to trust us and inspire them to improve." Let me illustrate with a personal experience.

When I was invited to work in U.S. President Ronald Reagan's White House as the premier speaker for Mrs. Nancy Reagan's "Just Say No" program, the original intent was to go into high schools, have the counselors identify the "at risk" students and teach them some tools to say no to alcohol and drugs. Thankfully, they responded to my sugges tion to turn it into a "Time Management Message" that would relate to the entire student body, with a message that if you are dreaming a good, clean, pure, powerful, positive, productive dream, and working hard on doing something positive, you won't have time to do something negative, and your positive actions will 'say no' for you!

Because this was one of the very first 'motivational school assemblies' in America, the requests from junior high/middle schools and elementary schools started flooding in. Consequently, between 1984 and 1989 I spoke in thousands of schools in all 50 states to millions of teenagers (in three schools every day, speaking on average to 6,000 students per day, for 140 school days each year, for six straight years in a row!)

Realizing that the 'Privilege of the Platform' is to 'bless, not impress,' and that our speaker's message must always be about the audience, my classic stories of 'Puppies For Sale,' the 'Circus,' and 'Jillair Jones' didn't relate as well to the those fourteen years of age and under and I needed to make an adjustment. The following commentary allowed me to immediately connect with the younger students by using an entertaining poem that related to them all:

"I remember when I got my first kiss – back in college – (pause to let them get it and laugh) and trying to figure out the technique to get another one! And at the time I couldn't figure out how going to math class could possibly help me become a professional football player. I failed to see the 'practical application.' Can any of you relate? Then one day it dawned on me. Mathematics is important. In fact, the sooner I mastered mathematics, the sooner I could start using it to make all of my dreams come true – including getting this next kiss, which was so important to me. This poem describes exactly what happened as I used mathematics to accomplish my goal. I'm sure the guys can relate. I call it "Mathematical Love":

He's teaching her arithmetic he said it was his mission
He kissed her once, he kissed her twice, and said, "Now that's addition"
And as he added smack by smack in silent satisfaction
She sweetly gave the kisses back and said,
"Now that's subtraction"
Then he kissed her, she kissed him, without an explanation Then
both together smiled and said, "That's multiplication"
Then dad appeared upon the scene and made a quick decision
He kicked that kid three blocks away and said,
"That's long division!"

(Copyright Dan Clark 1982)

THE ART OF SALES COMMUNICATION

There is also and obviously a communications system and formula to help sales professionals close more deals. My time-tested proven process I call "P-6."

Professional Performance skills + Persuasive Perception skills + Personality Positioning skills = Significant Sales results (Closing Most Sales)

In the corporate world, the sports and education worlds, and even in the military construct of rank advancement, we are hired for preparation, paid for performance, but promoted on potential. Which means the one activity all worlds share is selling. And because sale's is everybody's business, let me use this most honorable profession as the classic example of why and how Significant Selling and Marketing skills and tools are used:

Our acronym A.R.T. is the strategic template.

"P-6" (PPPPPP) is the tactical solution.

Developing and maintaining "skills" is the daily mission, with the dictionary definition of Skills being: specific proficiencies, talents, techniques, abilities and traits that are acquired and improved through training, that help you reach your full potential and set you apart from others.

Awareness: is about becoming completely literate in your "Professional Performance skills," which means you fully understand and commit to memory every fact, figure, product feature, service benefit, pricing structure, and relevant piece of information required for you to do your job. Having significant professional skills means you are an expert in every one of your products and services, well-educated on the most popular products and services of your top three competitors, know everything about the history of your industry, the history of your organization with its past and present leaders, and the reasons your company culture is unique and special. Because anybody can attain professional skills, this is only the "ticket" into the game.

The art of sales communication begins with perfecting your performance! Refinement: is about perfecting your Persuasive Perception skills," which are your sales skills. Because nobody likes to be sold, and everybody likes to buy what they want, you must learn and practice the organization's time-tested sales system until it becomes conversational so you can eloquently explain the practical application of your products and services.

Having significant persuasive skills means you are an expert in the art and science of asking the right questions so you can address the prospect's pain, overcome his/her objections, and create value by eliminating the pain and providing a real solution in an understandable, meaningful way. Bottom line? You never give a "sales pitch" and always present yourself as a trusted "problem solver" and advisor to help them not only get what they want, but most significantly, want what they get so they don't die with their music still in them!

Because the definition of sales is the "transference of trust," to accomplish this simple task you simply need to help your potential customer convert his/her needs to wants and why to how. The art of sales communication improves when you cultivate the right image!

Transformation: comes as you develop and continuously polish your "Personality Positioning skills," by working very hard on yourself not by working "on" your job, but working "in" your job. Alert! Having significant professional performance skills and persuasive perception skills do not make you a better person. Therefore, they are never as significant as personality positioning skills.

Having significant Personality skills means you have personal traits that make you stand out in every crowd, such as being: obedient, fearless, observant, impartial, independent, optimistic, intelligent, persistent, charming, precise, suave, meticulous, and trusting. Having significant positioning skills means you understand the short and long-term ramifications of visibility, visibility, visibility. Which means you are a master networker, going out of your way to connect with coworkers and prospective customers to develop trust, mutual respect, and loyalty "off task time" so on task time is more productive. The art of sales communication accelerates and closes more sales when you manage your exposure with the highest-level leaders and decision makers!

REWARDS OF FOLLOWING A SELLING SYSTEM

Significant Selling and Marketing high-performance productivity is accomplished through the simple but powerful process of 'duplication.' When sales professionals have a specific sales system and step-by-step process that they meticulously follow, they have a 93% chance of closing the sale. Without it, your chances of closing dramatically drop to 42%.

The same holds true when you follow a time-tested system and formula in your pursuit of the Art, Science and Spirit of a Significant Public Speaker And Storyteller.

CHAPTER FIVE

HOW DO YOU USE THE SYSTEMS?

ATTENTION, HOPE, ACTION

As you know, I am a professional speaker. My job is to teach, inspire, guide, push, and pull others to reach their full potential. Not to impress, but to bless and take others (and you) to a higher place than they can take themselves. Too many speakers and seminar leaders use "cutesy" shallow gimmicks, telling their listeners to "visualize" what they desire and to put a picture of the cruise ship vacation, sports car, elegant mansion, water ski boat, or whatever their dream may be, up on their refrigerator door. No, no, no!

To get what you want and, more important, become exactly who you want to be, don't visualize or look at the photo of the muscle-bound hunk or perfectly shaped super model. Visualize yourself going to the gym, sweating through the hard times, working out thirty minutes every morning no matter what. Visualize saying no to your second piece of cheesecake. Visualize making five more sales calls per week and coming to work early and staying late. In fact, to get yourself ready to fully embrace this last step-by-step formula, visualize the simple yet profound process that must be experienced before you can really change your life forever, improve yourself, and reduce chance from your everyday experience. I call this process the "Speaker's Triangle."

The Art and Science of Significant Public Speaking begins with the understanding of only one reality: in order for an audience member to open up his/her mind and heart, truly listen to what the presenter is sharing, and unconditionally trust the facts and feelings he/she is experiencing, each of us must get the answers to three categorical questions. Regardless if we are only one person riding in the car of a realtor, a participant in a small business group listening to the presentation of a Financial Advisor, or one of several thousand attendees at a huge convention, we all are asking three questions:

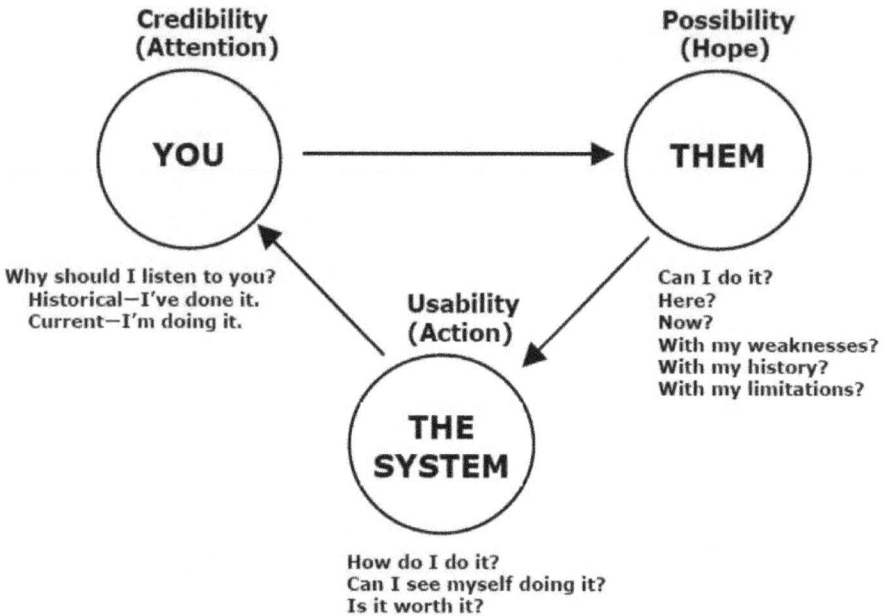

Credibility (Attention)

Possibility (Hope)

YOU

THEM

Why should I listen to you?
Historical—I've done it.
Current—I'm doing it.

Usability (Action)

Can I do it?
Here?
Now?
With my weaknesses?
With my history?
With my limitations?

THE SYSTEM

How do I do it?
Can I see myself doing it?
Is it worth it?

Speaker, author, seminar facilitator, life coach, or organizational leader needs to answer the number one question, or there won't be a second one. Every audience member needs and deserves to know: "Why should I listen to you?" The answer builds the necessary credibility to get the listener's, reader's, or employee's attention. Through further illustrations, documented research, and inspirational stories, the speaker can speak with authority and give hope that their audience can also do what they have done. Only now will they believe strongly enough to take action and use the system in their lives because they know it is worth it.

WHY SHOULD I LISTEN TO YOU?

People relate to our "imperfections" not our perfections (if we even have any!) Our audience members don't give a 'rat's wah-ka-zoodle' if we have ever succeeded. They want to know, "Did you ever fail? Have you ever been knocked down and broken, and what did you do about it?"

Because the definition of sales is the 'transference of trust;' and because the art of public speaking and storytelling is nothing more than 'selling' our ideas and solutions, the most important part of establishing our 'credibility' requires that we first be "ordinary" to connect with the audience about something they have done. Only then have we established enough 'trust' in our credibility for us to share why we are "extraordinary" by sharing something they have not done.

Because the goal in every speech and presentation is NOT to have the audience members leave impressed with you, but rather, to have them leave being more impressed with themselves, aware of their potential, and inspired to become more of who they already are, as speakers we must first connect physically, mentally and emotionally. Remember, 'credibility' is not as much about what you have done and accomplished, as it is about who you are as an extraordinary, inspirational, role model human being!

CAN I DO IT TOO?

I am often asked who is my favorite speaker? This is definitely a tough question because my mentors Zig Ziglar and Art Berg come to mind. However, the two speakers who stand out the most are two war heroes by the names of Captain Gerry Coffee, and Captain Charlie Plumb – both of whom were shot down in the Vietnam War and held in Hỏa Lò Prison (the Hanoi Hilton) for 6 to 7 years in solitary confinement.

Art Berg was a successful entrepreneur and extraordinary human being who was paralyzed in an automobile accident that left him a quadriplegic.

Art was the most powerful speaker I have ever met whose stories and sense of humor convinced everybody who met him and heard him that life is a choice – that it's more than cliché' to say it's not what happens to us, but what we do with what happens to us that defines who we are.

After Art finishes his speech no one could ever feel sorry for themselves, and everyone leaves believing that if we were paralyzed, we too could and would and should go on and become a world-class athlete, husband, father, and wealthy businessman.

It was an honor to sing at Art's funeral and I miss our weekly interaction every day. Sadly, there is a speaker on the circuit who is also paralyzed and in a wheelchair who is telling some of Art's famous stories as if they are his own. I wish he had integrity enough to let him rest in peace!

Captains Coffee and Plumb were tortured beyond belief and yet returned to their cell every time with dignity and honor and eventually returned to America with dignity and honor. In Coffee's book, "Beyond Survival," he shares that it was Faith in God, Faith in Country, Faith in Family, and Faith in Self that helped him survive and thrive. And why does this make him one of the greatest speakers in the world? Because when you leave his speech, you actually believe that had you been shot down and tortured beyond belief, that you too, would have survived and thrived and returned with honor, by focusing on the same four beliefs that he had!

Captain Charlie Plumb also and obviously returned with dignity and honor and chronicled his brutal experience in his book, "I'm No Hero." His story is equally compelling but Charlie adds an experience to his speech that increases his ROI with an immediate "Call To Action," which solicits an immediate answer from every listener, "Yes, I can and I SHOULD do it too!

A while ago I had Charlie as a guest on my weekly radio show and asked him to tell the following story. With his permission I am sharing it here:

When Charlie had been home from the war for a while, he and his wife were out to dinner where a man started tarring at him from across the restaurant. Finally, he spoke up and said, "You're Captain Charlie Plumb who flew jets off the Kitty Hawk Carrier in the Vietnam War."

Startled and curious, Charlie admitted that yes he was, and asked him how he knew that. The man proudly replied, "I packed your parachute the day you got shot down."

With tears in his eyes Charlie stood, shook his hand and hugged him with a giant "thank you." The man then confessed, "Everyday I did the same boring thing and never felt like my job mattered. At least not until you got shot down. I guess the shoot worked, eh?"

Plumb laughed, agreed, and again expressed his gratitude, sitting down with a lump in his throat with the overwhelming guilt of how many times he must have walked past this young man on the ship and never said hello, or asked how he was – because Charlie was a cocky, cool, invincible fighter pilot, and he was just a lowly blue collar sailor.

In his speech, Charlie then asks his audience, "Who packed your chute today?"

On the very first time I shared the speaker's platform with Charlie, I walked away never to be the same! And to this day, I ask myself, which out of sight, "parachute packing" person has helped me physically, mentally, spiritually, emotionally, socially, financially and with my family today?

By the time Charlie finishes his speech, every audience member has a clear answer to "Can I Do I Too?" with an understanding that not only do THEIR "Parachute Packers" exist, but it's now their responsibility to leave the meeting committed to always remember the 'little guy,' to cheer on the underdog, generously tip taxi drivers, and airport skycaps, and hotel bellman and restaurant wait staff, thank hotel housekeepers, and forever live with an attitude of gratitude for everybody and everything!

I have heard the speeches of adventurers who climbed Mount Everest, with breathtaking photos and tales of near death experiences, but because I have no desire to climb a 29,000 foot mountain, it had no real relevance to my life, and I only left the speech entertained.

However, had he related his climb to my daily struggles, which are "Everest's" to me, and explained exactly how he prepared himself physically and mentally, and why it was important for him to first climb to the base camp before he continued, and what specific steps he took each day to achieve his goal, I would have left believing that I too, can climb my personal Everest's.

"SEEK TO BLESS – NOT IMPRESS" IRON COWBOY

Because I coached my good friend James Lawrence, the Iron Cowboy, and helped him tweak and take his speech to the next level, I am familiar with a particular story within his story:

James set the most incredible world record in Extreme Sports and Endurance, by completing 50 Ironman competitions, in 50 consecutive days, in each of the 50 states, tells the story of a woman who wanted to run the last five K of his 26.2 mile marathon portion of the Ironman because she had struggled with obesity her entire life. She came out in North Dakota on his day 45 and was the very last person to finish. As she crossed the finish line he went up to her and asked, "How was that?" She said, "It's the hardest thing I've ever done." What she said next surprised him. She smiled and asked, "Can I do it again tomorrow?"

James agreed to welcome her but told her she had to travel to South Dakota. Sure enough, she showed up, again finished last in the final 5 K, and was again asked, "How was it?" And again she answered, "It was the hardest thing she's ever done, and could she do it again tomorrow?"

For five consecutive days she showed up, took action and did the work. The point? This is a good story the way it is. But it becomes a great story that teaches a powerful life-affirming motivational message when you add the "moral to the story," which is Her Hard Was No Different Than James's Hard! They were equally tough for where they were on their individual journeys.

James's hard was 50 Ironman's in 50 days. Her's was 5, 5k's in 5 days. Your hard might be waking up today and taking the first step to start your day. It doesn't matter. Remember – the goal as a speaker is to bless, not impress, and to make sure that every audience member believes that he/she can do what you have done!

"THE SYSTEM" HOW DO I DO IT – WHAT DO I DO NOW?

As we will eventually discuss in detail, crafting an extraordinary speech that 'listener's love' includes the presentation of three major points. We are all accustomed to hearing three points – a list of two subconsciously makes us feel like you forgot something – four points are too many and subconsciously make us feel overwhelmed! Captain Coffee effectively follows this time-tested formula in his book, 'Beyond Survival' and in each of his keynote speeches by stating that he survived because of 'Faith In God and Country, Faith In Family, and Faith In Self.'

Bottom line. It's always a great idea to tie your closing 'takeaway' assignment into some 'catchy quotes' that are easy to remember – powerful quips they can 'hang their hat on' and take home with them. For example, I personally use:

"Today you've never been this old before – and today you'll never be this young again – so right now, and every 'right now' matters! Which means no matter what your past has been you have a spotless future.

Which means you can't always control what happens, but you can always control what happens next!"

With this 'set up' you now answer the third question by *recapping* the three points you have presented during your speech, and converting them into a list of Three Actionable Items they can immediately start working on when they leave your presentation. This is the ROI 'Return On Investment' that both the meeting planner and each audience member are expecting. This is when you bring your listeners full circle and teach them the step-by-step proven process that answers the questions that connected you to them in the first place: "Did you ever fail? How can I also adapt to change, be resilient, and with my weaknesses, limitations and strengths, what is the 'system' that will take me from where I am to where I want to be?"

CHAPTER SIX

WHO ARE YOU REALLY?
YOU ARE THE MESSAGE!

When it comes to becoming a consummate public speaker six foundational truths set an uncompromising expectation that each of us should embrace:

- The only person I need to be better than is the person I was yesterday. We human beings are hard-wired for progress and personal development. Inspired people don't have to be motivated!

- The definition of sales in the 'transference of trust.' We must be unshakeable in our integrity, constant in our service before self and continuous in our commitment to excellence in everything we do.

- To kill a king we must be a king. In order to be invited to associate with the most powerful and influential (politically, socially) and have access to their inner circles of influence, we must become one of them (physically, intellectually, financial ly, ethically, spiritually).

- The goal is not to do business with everybody who wants what you have. The goal is to do business only with those who believe what you believe, so they choose you, not just somebodywho does what you do.

- It is not enough to practice what we preach – we must preach only what we practice, so we are predictable and the same on and off stage!

- Seek to bless, not impress, so everyone always leaves you saying, "I like me best when I'm with you, I want to see you again!'

For this reason, this chapter is presented as a 'man-in-the-mirror' self audit experience that allows you to embellish your answer to the first Speakers Triangle question: Why Should Anybody Listen To You? by answering the deeper questions: Are you inspiring to listen to and fascinating to be around? Are you continuously becoming everything you were born to be so your resume is different this month and improved over last year? Clearly, you are the message! Who are you really?

YOLANDA

Yolanda was hired at a corporation as the administrative assistant to the CEO. She was exceptionally qualified and immediately received a raise for her outstanding work. One evening the executive team, including her boss, was attending an NBA basketball game. Unbeknownst to them, she had auditioned and was selected to sing the National Anthem. Before she had even finished the song, the crowd began to cheer and continued to cheer and stomp and whistle and clap for at least two minutes afterward. Truly she had blown everyone's mind, and people commented, "As good as Whitney Houston and Jennifer Hudson" and "the next Beyoncé."

To deepen my illustration, have you ever heard Celine Dion sing "God Bless America" and she's a French Canadian? Amazing! Breathtaking! But only when you hear a National Karaoke Champion sing the same song, do you understand the difference between a super star multi-platinum recording artist who performs the song and someone who merely sings the music.

Question: Was Yolanda an administrative assistant who happened to be a phenomenal superstar performing artist, or was Yolanda a superstar performing artist who happened to be an administrative assistant? What natural talent were you born with that ignites your passionate purpose and drives you to wake up early and stay up late, and that you would do even if you didn't get paid to do it?

Who are you – really? You definitely were born to be you you'd make a lousy somebody else! So why settle for just being successful and getting only what you want, when you could live a life of significance and want what you get so that you don't die with your music still in you? The successful teach and generate followers. The significant inspire and lead and create more leaders! Successful speakers are merely polished 'presenters' with an emphasis on what they do. Significant speakers are professional communication 'connectors' with an emphasis on who they really are and who they were born to be!

KING LOUIS XVI

When Louis the XVI was forced from his throne and imprisoned, his young son, the prince, was kidnapped by those who overthrew the kingdom. They thought that inasmuch as the king's son was heir to the throne, if they could destroy him morally, he wouldn't realize the great and grand destiny that life had bestowed upon him.

Consequently, they took him to a community far away and exposed the boy to every filthy and vile thing that life could offer. They exposed him to foods that would quickly make him a slave to appetite, continuously used vulgar language around him, and constantly exposed him to lewd and lusting women, alcohol, dishonor and distrust.

For over six months he was bombarded twenty-four hours a day by everything that could drag the soul of a man into wickedness, rude, crude, defiled and unrefined behavior. But never once did the young prince buckle under pressure. Finally, his captors gave up on tempting and changing him and asked why had he not submitted himself to partaking of these worldly pleasures to satisfy his most lustful desires that were his for the taking.

With a deep and confident sense of self, the boy proudly and humbly answered, "I cannot do what you ask, for I was born to be a king!"

"DAN CLARK'S BALANCE WHEEL"

(The Ultimate Self Audit)

Come to grips with the reality that no matter where you go, there you are; mere geographic relocation doesn't change much of anything. Now evaluate this "Balance Wheel" diagram combining nine aspects and areas of our lives:

Rating yourself on a scale of 1 to 15 (15 being the highest level of performance), ponder how fully you've been living in the nine areas. Do you purposefully take care of your body? Do your keep your mind active? How fully have you been nurturing your soul with charitable deeds? Do you experience on a daily basis the vital emotions of fear, pain, joy, love, peace, and satisfaction? Do you approach your work with an eye toward always learning something new? Because no other success can compensate for failure in the home, and quantity time has a quality all of its own, can your family see that they are the most important thing in the world to you?

Mark the boxes that reflect how you feel you are currently performing, and draw a line to connect your number on the scale with each of the nine categories until it makes some version of a circle.

Physical Fitness

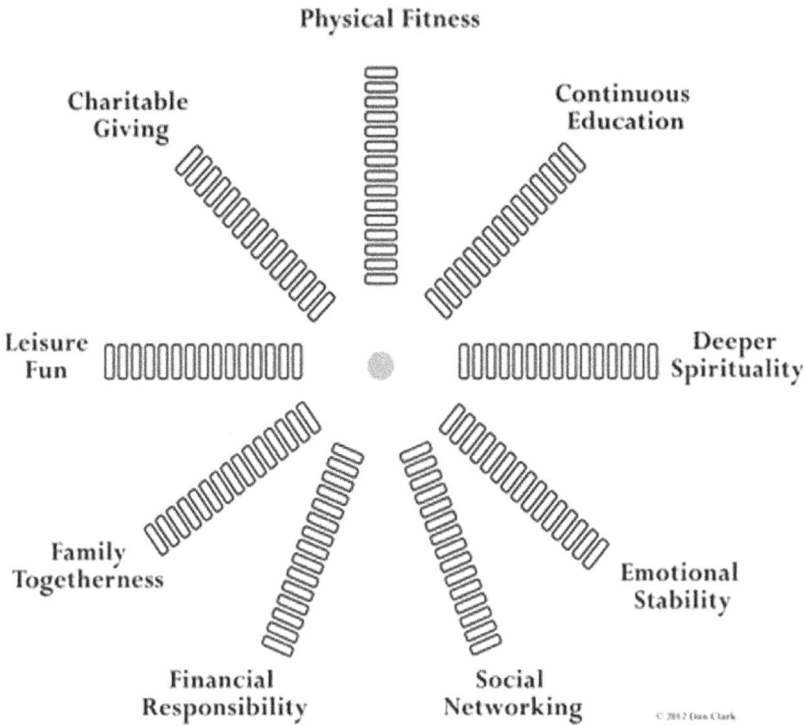

Charitable Giving — Continuous Education — Leisure Fun — Deeper Spirituality — Family Togetherness — Emotional Stability — Financial Responsibility — Social Networking

© 2012 Dan Clark

This wheel is now a snapshot of your life in or out of balance. Which parts of your life are working best right now: body, mind, spirit, emotions, friends, family, career, or finances? Where can you improve, not all at once, but one box, one day, one quality, one attribute, one task at a time?

Remember, when our lives get tough and our ride seems rough and bumpy, most blame the road. But in reality, it is us we need to fix. Once we balance and round out our wheel, the ride is smooth, and the way is rewarding. For today and for every day after, each time you stretch and improve one number and one single step on the Balance Wheel scale, commit yourself in writing to sustaining this extraordinary thinking and fresh behavior until it becomes a new habit and personal pattern. Write your first goal here and commit to taking action today, to improve in some small and significant way.

Remember: the only person you need to be better than is the person you were yesterday!

Physical Fitness

_____

_____

Continuous Education

_____

_____

Deeper Spirituality

_____

_____

Emotional Stability

_____

_____

Social Networking

_____

_____

Financial Responsibility

_____

_____

Family Togetherness

_____

_____

Leisure Fun

_____

_____

Charitable Giving

_____

_____

THE 'THERMOSTAT'

A thermostat is an instrument that focuses on inside conditions, measuring changes in circumstances that allow us to accurately predict and expect what the temperature will be. A thermostat is a component of an HVAC (heating and air conditioning) control system that senses the difference between actual temperature and desired set-point temperature. It switches heating and cooling devices on and off to maintain a desired temperature. The moment you set the thermostat, it triggers a heater or air conditioner to run at full capacity until the set-point temperature is reached. Then it shuts off the equipment until it's needed again.

In terms of our human set point, it is always dialed into the level of our self-esteem, sense of self-worth, and degree of personal development.

For example, how many times have we seen someone win 100 million dollars in the lottery only to be flat broke three years later? How many people do we know who go on a crazy diet and lose fifty pounds or more, but six months later they have gained all the weight back and more. Why is this?

It is simply because of their personal thermostat. No matter what happens on the outside with money, weight, relationships, promotions of authority, and so forth, ultimately our thermostat is going to kick in to bring our outside world to match our internal set point. In order to accumulate more in the outside world, the key to this equation is to become more on the inside. Who are you – Really? Who do you need to be in order to inspire, teach, guide and lead others through word and deed?

CHAPTER SEVEN

ARE YOU SOMEONE WORTH LISTENING TO ON AND OFF STAGE?

A professional speaker spends less time preparing a speech and more time preparing himself to speak. A professional presenter gets his credibility from the speech content and slick delivery. It is memorized and presented with the attitude that it's easier to change the audience than it is to change the speech. Consequently, a professional presenter thinks the time in front of his audience is about him instead of about them. Conversations between professional presenters usually include confessions like, "Wow, the audience loved me on Friday. But on Tuesday, at my other meeting, they were stupid—didn't get half my jokes or relate to me at all."

How shallow is this? It's like showing up to a dinner party and pulling out three by five cards with your conversation written out on them and engaging the people at your table only in a planned, practiced, non-spontaneous way, void of sincerity, two-way nonverbal communication, and authentic connection. The only place from which a person can grow is where he is. You must follow your audience physically and emotionally. Only there can you gently invite them to buy into your message. It is the secret to sales, customer service, coaching, parenting, human resource management, leadership, teaching, and public speaking.

Because of this, the purpose of a meeting is to take the audience members on an emotional, thought-provoking roller coaster ride to a higher place than they can take themselves and to give them a deeper experience than they can get at home or work. How dare anyone, especially a professional presenter, adulterate their opportunity to touch someone's life by taking their privilege of the platform so lightly? If the presentation is about PowerPoint illustrations, videos, graphs, or information, doesn't it seem completely ridiculous to bring people together at great travel and time expense just to have someone stand up in front of them to rattle off some cookie-cutter presentation that could have been emailed to everyone individually?

Professional presenters tell, teach, and coach other wannabe professional presenters to find the person in the audience who is smiling and nodding in total agreement and then to feed off that person throughout their entire speech. No, no, no! These are the folks who also tell you to come from backstage when you are introduced.

Again, no. Always sit in the back of the room to get a reality check on the emotional state of those who don't want to be there. When you are introduced, you have ample time to get to the stage. Then, when onstage, immediately start looking for the youngest and oldest male and female and the most negative male and female who disagree with you. The challenge and reward of your speech then becomes to relate to each of them, to truly connect and positively touch their lives, knowing that if they get it, everyone else has as well.

PREPARING YOURSELF TO SPEAK

Don't trust your memory. When you hear an extraordinary joke, immediately write it down. Always carry a small, pocket-sized notebook around with you. You never know when you're going to see or hear a powerful quotable quote, hear something funny, witness a unique metaphor or analogy for successful living, or participate in a significant emotional experience—you can't afford to forget the intimate details that touched your soul forever.

Why my emphasis on extraordinary bellyaching jokes, powerful perfectly worded quotable quotes, and eyewitness personal accounts? Because these are the key ingredients of an extraordinary, entertaining, thought-provoking, unique, inspirational speech that allow you to speak with authority. Being able to share your own observations, analogies, and life-changing experiences is what turns a professional presenter into a professional speaker and puts you in demand.

Finding and developing your own stories comes through simple self-audited, self-administered question and answer sessions. Some ideas include thinking about your first job interview, first date, being fired, parenting, traffic tickets, vacation or travel screw-ups, embarrassing moments, family holidays, changing your first diaper, and so forth. With passion, creativity, and imagination, the sky is the limit.

What makes a professional speaker uniquely different and in high demand, and what allows a professional speaker to command a much higher speaker's honorarium than a professional presenter, is not the content and slick delivery of the speech while he is onstage. It is everything he has thought and experienced, and it is the person he has become long before he came onstage. It's being exactly the same offstage as you are onstage.

Speaking professionally is not putting on a show. The speech doesn't give you credibility; your life does! Being a professional speaker is about sharing the hours and years of incredible experiences, responsibilities, failures, and successes that you amassed before you began your speech. And even though you only have a 60-minute time slot in which to impart your wisdom. Your audience sees, feels, and senses your depth, character, and the library of knowledge that is left unspoken.

Professional speakers have so much more to say and give that oftentimes they are invited back to speak to the same audience again. Professional speakers should always come across as the tip of the iceberg—the audience should feel that they have only heard the surface, only 10 percent of the huge, wide, solid iceberg beneath.

Bottom line reality? Every speech should inspire and persuade. This means every informational or educational speech should not be a speech at all. It should be an email, fax, or letter. If you want me to remember facts and figures, you must give them to me in written form so that I can read, ponder, read again, study, and internalize them over time. However, if you want us to improve, increase our productivity, and become more of who we are, then gather us all together that we may see who our leaders are and, in turn, allow them to earn the required respect from us that gives them the right to the title of leader.

STORY POWER

The greatest compliment anyone can pay me as a professional speaker is to call me a master storyteller. Stories work by connecting concepts and facts with feelings. When you merely mention important ideas to an audience, they may agree with their importance. But not many will remember the specifics because to the audience, they are cold, hard, and distant. You have offered them no personal or intimate reason to remember your points. However, wrap those same concepts in a stimulating, emotional story, and not one of them will forget the story or the ideas associated with it.

Speaker coach Max Dixon gave this advice: "Continue to develop the 'story-ness' of your presentation. Share stories of victory and not victimization, suiting length of the story to importance of point. A well-crafted, well-told story can create exceptional rapport with any audience, especially if you utilize the emotional power of words to paint pictures: 'a tonic of opportunity,' 'an embracing development,' 'just let that idea relax by the fire until it feels like talking,' and so forth."

In our storytelling we should carefully select words that best shape the space we are describing such as suffocating relationship, intoxicating conversation, claustrophobic cubicle. In a single crafted sentence, the right words can evoke memories and associations with our senses of smell and taste (the very mention of "cinnamon" stimulates a real sensory effect). It can also conjure up vivid images that invite the attendees to actively participate in defining the image you are creating, for instance, "what are your sounds of silence?"

The story is the "for instance," or illustrative example, that binds the point with the proof and the idea to the listener's bottom-line belief. Give me an idea—complex or simple, deeply philosophical or cognitively scientific—while you have me laughing or crying, and I will always remember your speech and never forget your lesson!

REAL LIFE ROCKY

Sylvester Stallone is the perfect example of someone who looked in his own life for an inspirational story that could help others. Let me share the inspirational story behind the Rocky movie series. Stallone, through fate or circumstance, ended up at the Muhammad Ali versus Chuck Wepner heavyweight fight. Wepner, a battling, bruising type of club fighter who had never really made the big time, was now having his shot. But the fight was not regarded as a serious battle. It was called a public joke. He would barely go three rounds, most of the predictions said.

Well, the history books will read that he went fifteen rounds and established himself as one of the few men who had ever gone the distance with Muhammad Ali. Stallone later wrote that that night must have meant more to Wepner than any money he could have ever received from fighting because now he had run the complete circle. It was the reason he had been training for thirty-four years.

At that time Sylvester Stallone was a starving "nobody" actor with a dream to write a movie script. That fight was the inspiration for his main character. He was going to create Rocky Balboa, a man from the streets, a walking cliché of sorts, the all-American tragedy, a man who didn't have much mentally but had incredible emotion, patriotism, spirituality, and good nature, even though nature had not been good to him.

With his lead character identified, he then needed a specific story line for the movie, which turned out to be Stallone's own personal story of his inability to be recognized, looking only for a break to show what he could do. So, Stallone took his own predicament and injected it into the character of Rocky because no one, he felt, would be interested in a story about a down-and-out, struggling actor and writer.

But Rocky Balboa was different. He was America's child. He was to the seventies what Charlie Chaplin's Little Tramp was to the twenties.

What some do not know is that the catch in Stallone's sales pitch to the film production companies was that Stallone came with the script. If they wanted to make the movie, Sylvester would definitely be playing the lead part and star as Rocky. The rest is history— Academy Award for Best Picture, followed by five sequel *Rocky* movies released in subsequent years with the final *Rocky VI* in 2006 to complete the enormously successful series. In a nutshell, Sylvester Stallone faced his fears and didn't just let life come to him; he came to life. He conceived, he believed, and because he planned his work and worked his plan, he achieved exactly what he set out to do.

Bottom line? This story was there. All Stallone had to do was stop his hectic life long enough to figure out what the story was. You and I can and should do the same! Countless stories occur in our personal and professional lives all around us. We need only find them, define their meaning and purpose, capture them in writing, practice telling them, and add them to our repertoire as speakers.

I did it with my previously shared story "Puppies for Sale," that was made into a short film at Paramount Studios starring the late Jack Lemmon and ten-year-old Jesse James. Another story I wrote that same year is called 'The Circus,' which is a tender 'service-before-self' story about my dad and me buying tickets to go to the circus. Both stories have become international favorites in the *Chicken Soup for the Soul* series and came as a result of me looking for the stories going on in my life and figuring out what lessons they taught.

DEVELOPING YOUR UNIQUE FACTOR

You cannot be an inspirational speaker if what you did that makes you inspirational is yesterday's news. The reason my message is fresh is because I am. I am always creating opportunities to push myself with the belief that no matter what my past has been, I have a spotless future. Your 'Unique Factor' is different than your 'Signature Story,' which is the one Significant Emotional Experience (S.E.E.) in your life that gives you the right to be a professional speaker.

I am talking about always going for the gusto and doing extraordinary things that don't regularly occur in ordinary life. I am talking about reading one book a week for the last thirteen years (I have) and attending special concerts and historic events that will give you experiences to share. I am always looking to develop relationships by giving much more than I take so these relationships can pay off someday if the opportunity presents itself. Because of this mentality, my unique factor in the market is: 'I wonder what cool thing Dan has done this year. I wonder what big name celebrity Dan has interviewed this month. I can't wait to have Dan back to demonstrate to our people that we shouldn't let ourselves get stale or stagnant!'

If a person's resume is the same this year as it was last year, shame on that lazy, non-passionate, non-creative, non-imaginative person who is stuck in their past. We must commit to being lifelong learners, to taking calculated risks into areas that teach us things we cannot learn from PowerPoint presentations and books. This is why we need speakers. We must always remember that the purpose of a meeting is to give someone an experience they can't get at home or work and to take them to a place they cannot take themselves.

To do this, the speaker must have already done it in his own life! Make a list of amazing things you want to do. After you experience each one, it is easy to figure out what you learned from it. This becomes another arrow in your quiver, another club in your golf bag of stories you can choose from to help you customize your remarks.

HAIR ON FIRE

I have flown most of the fighter jets in the United States Air Force and Navy including the T-38, F-4, F-15, F-16, and F-18, with each sortie lasting 90 minutes, and the commander in each aircraft allowing me to take the stick and fly the plane for 30 minutes! Whoa! Question: Do I tell the stories for entertainment? No. I share them as illustrations of significant leadership principles, and leveled-up self-development beliefs.

For example, when I flew an F-15, the control stick is straddled between your knees. It moves three inches forward, three inches to the left and right, and five inches backward. You need only move that control stick one inch in either one of those four directions and it completely changes the entire direction of the aircraft forty-five degrees. Message? Small deliberate change makes a huge difference, and "the little things really do matter—yes we should sweat the small stuff!' And now, because of the prior research I did on the organization, I can give them specific examples of small changes they could make as individuals and as an organization.

I flew an F-16 with the Air Force Thunderbirds, performing every air-show maneuver, flying in formation with other jets, catching 9.4 Gs at Mach speed. The F-16 does not have a floor-mounted control stick, but rather a control grip mounted on the right side of the cockpit. It is a 'fly-by-wire' system where the grip only moves three eighths of an inch. You can't even tell you are moving it. When we landed, I interviewed the Lead Thunderbird pilot who taught me about Trust, and that preparation is what creates confidence in self and from others.

You see, the other three pilots flying in the famous 'diamond formation' don't fly looking ahead and at their instruments. Each of them only looks at the Lead jet and follows the Lead pilot's directions. They are putting 100% total trust in another person, realizing trust is created and strengthened off task, off duty, off work, and during practice, not during the air show.

When I share this story with my audiences, I teach the powerful truth that, 'Under pressure you don't rise to the occasion. You fall to your level of training. That's why we train and practice and prepare so hard!'

The lesson I learned flying the F-18 is even more profound. When we landed, I asked the pilot how we flew this incredible machine. He said, 'By Feel.' I asked him to explain. He said, 'You become the plane,' and continued asking by me, 'When you climbed up the ladder to slide into the cockpit, did you strap yourself into the F-18, or did you strap the F-18 onto you?'

Think about this. You don't fly a high-performance jet with the cognitive, analytical, informational left side of the brain. You go supersonic and push the jet, yourself and your organization to the highest level of peak performance with the creative, emotional, touchy, feely, relational right side of your brain!

Check out my website at danclark.com. Who knows? Perhaps I can be a source of inspiration. Remember, a true professional speaker only uses his own material and the cool, exhilarating, once-in-a-lifetime experiences he has had to illustrate his points. What will be your 'Unique Factor?'

CHAPTER EIGHT

SO... YOU WANT TO GET PAID TO SPEAK?

JOB, CAREER, OR CALLING

When I was paralyzed playing football, the doctors told me I wouldn't recover, but recover I did. As I got better, I was asked to speak. Through 100 percent referrals, more I spoke, the more I was asked to speak. Through 100 percent referrals, I parlayed speaking into a full-time profession, averaging over 150 full-fee speaking engagements annually since 1982.

My point? I didn't choose speaking as my career; it chose me. Without flattering myself, I had a message and an experience that people wanted to hear and learn from and the phone just kept ringing. For this reason, I cringe when someone comes to me and says they have decided they want to become a professional speaker. Others may disagree, but I believe professional speaking is not something anyone can choose. Being a professional speaker is a "calling."

For some reason, you have been singled out and "knighted" to serve a mission for humanity. Your purpose is larger than making money—you truly believe you are on this earth and have been given certain experiences that you may share with others to help bring peace, goodwill, love, success, and extraordinary achievement to your fellow beings. This is why I ask wannabes, "What is your message?" Not what do they think the market is looking for, or what is the current buzzword, or popular topic of the month. What do they know to be true from their own experience that they feel honored, compelled, and committed to share with everyone who will listen?

If you feel you have been "called" to be a professional speaker, here are the three questions you must ask and answer and the one next step you must take to turn your calling into reality: What would you drive five hours one-way to say to somebody? What is your specific message? Who would benefit from your message? This identifies your market (students, educators, athletes, sales professionals, customer service agents, military, doctors, government employees, IT). Where does your market meet? This identifies your marketing location (schools, trade association conventions, corporate training meetings, sales rallies). Do what is necessary to get your name and message in front of the decision-makers and get booked on their programs. The one next step you should take is to join the National Speakers Association and become an active member.

THE 3 MS OF SPEAKING PROFESSIONALLY

M 1: Message

Quantifying your Message begins by answering some introspective soul-searching questions: What is your real motivation – to make money or make a difference? Why do you care? Why is this message or idea important to you? Why should your audience listen to you? What is your true mission? What do you want your audience to know, do, feel, or believe? What transformation do you offer? What do you want to accomplish? In one sentence, what is your message? Can you make it memorable? Repeatable? Which brings up the most frequently asked questions: how do you determine your message?

Some things are true whether you believe them or not. Everybody is entitled to his/her own opinion, but nobody is entitled to the wrong facts. Right is right. Period. There are certain universal, time-tested, natural laws and proven principles that have always been around, that are always at work, and always right. Gravity was

69

at work long before the apple conked Newton on the head. You don't win with the best players; you win with the right players. "Best" is comparing yourself to *who* is right and based on competition against others. "Right" is comparing yourself to a higher standard of performance, ethics, core values, and success principles based on *what* is right. Right is truth and is not voted on, or made policy because majority rules. Right and truth are correct all by themselves or together in the cosmos.

Why do I bring this up? When anyone asks me to help them become a professional speaker, I always ask them one question: "What would you drive five hours one-way to say to someone if it wasn't for a loved one and you were not being paid for your speech?" If their answer is that they wouldn't, then I politely tell them they don't have what it takes to be a professional speaker. One of the things I am most proud of is the fact that over thirty years I have missed only one speech. This is with over 5,500 audiences in all fifty states and 75 foreign countries. My missed speech was because I was taken to the emergency room and the doctors wouldn't let me leave the hospital in time to fly from Los Angeles to Massachusetts.

I've had planes cancel and weather delays and airports close, but I have always scrambled. Many times, I have run through airports to catch a different airline just leaving, chartered King Airs and Lear Jets at my own expense, and rented cars to drive several hours just to keep my commitments. I don't know if I'm the greatest speaker on the planet, but guaranteed I am always going to show up! Meeting Planners know it – my reputation is solid! My message is clear, and I need to share it with the world.

So why have I not missed speeches? Why have I driven five hours one-way to speak for free? Because I've been way down, and I honestly believe that I really do know how others feel and that my message will help them heal.

Once you honestly admit that you are called to be a professional speaker (much like a priest and preacher feel called into the ministry), it is time to start focusing on your message. Although you know a lot about a lot of things, the easiest way to get focused on this bottom-line message is to do two things:

First, ponder the following list of superficial questions that will get your juices flowing and fill in your answers:

List two favorite hobbies:

_____

_____

List one positive and one negative childhood memory:

_____

_____

List one positive and one negative adult experience (fell in love/broken heart – got the job/didn't get the job):

_____

_____

List two very personal adult experiences:

_____

_____

List two core values:

_____

_____

List two mighty dreams:

_____

_____

List two realistic goals:

_____

_____

List two current events:

_____

_____

List two social problems that interest you:

_____

_____

List two controversial issues:

_____

_____

List two things you want to be remembered for after you die:

_____

_____

Social Networking

_____

_____

Social Networking

_____

_____

Second, orchestrate a personal soul-baring event, followed by an introspective exercise in writing your 'Last Lecture' by answering whatyou would say to someone if you knew you only had one hour to live.

This 'soul-baring' event is an interview with yourself, conducted by someone who can and will ask you deep, compelling, thought-provoking questions. They will prick your memories, connect you to yourpast, energize your recall, and stir your emotions to vent and dump and 'throw up' every good and bad experience you can possibly thinkof from as far back as you can remember.

Do not try to figure out the lesson you learned or attempt to philosophize about why the experience occurred. This is a simple five-hourinterview with the sole purpose of capturing and writing down your personal history and reminiscing about every possible person, place, and thing that has ever influenced your life.

We should not spend time on writing a speech until we have spent enough time preparing ourselves to speak. Therefore, this interviewis not focused on writing a speech on a specific subject that seems to be a popular topic of the day that meeting planners are paying peopleto speak about. This interview is for you to simply talk about growingup, your family influences and crazy experiences with your siblings, your neighborhood, sports, recreational activities, hobbies, vacations, sacrifices, service projects, heroes and why, villains and people you despise and why, amazing successes, horrible failures, great relationships and love, first kiss, first job, lost loves, lost jobs, broken hearts, shattered dreams, dreams that came true, and especially your "SEE" experiences that psychologists refer to as our "Significant Emotional Events."

You can record this interview on a digital device and use a software program or hire someone to transcribe it to create a typewrittendocument. Or you can do what I do when I write a speech for someone and hire a professional 'Court Reporter,' who will come to your home and take notations as you interact and talk with your interviewer, who then presents you with a typed out document as soon as the session is over.

Once you have thoroughly captured every memory you can possibly think of in your physical, mental, spiritual, emotional, social, financial, familial, and charitable worlds, and you have it in a double-spaced typewritten document, identify a college English professoror a Hall of Fame professional speaker like myself who is officially qualified and genuinely interested in helping you write a speech. Yes, it will cost you money to hire him/her or me, but here is where your investment (which you will get back in your first few paid speaking engagements) will help you make the transition from a wannabe polished presenter who tells other people's stories and uses other people'smaterial, to being a true professional speaker who only tells your ownstories and uses your own material.

At this point in the process you hire us as your non-emotional compiler, organizer, editor, or writer who has no attachment to any of your stories. We can read through your five-hour interview transcript, evaluate your thoughts and experiences to tell you what you are a subject expert in, and what specific topic you are most passionate about and most qualified to talk about.

Remember, the first question in the Speaker's Triangle is: "Why Should I Listen To You?" This is the "credibility" piece, which audience members need to answer before they let you proceed with your speech. It's obvious when someone is pretending to be someone they are not. We have no credibility onstage and/or in a boardroom or vehicle delivering a sales presentation unless we are the same offstage and/or out of the conference center or car. It is not enough to just practice what we preach – we must preach only what we practice!

That's right. Because we need to spend most of our time preparingourselves to speak, instead of you telling yourself what you are an expert in (which is usually distorted by our preconceived desire to speakabout a specific topic), it is critical that you hire an expert interviewer who can capture your true essence, character, passion, purpose, priorities, and personality—who has written many speeches for him/ herself and others and knows what to do with your newly created personal history. Call me! 800-676-1121.

Once you know what you are an expert in, position yourself not as a professional speaker, but rather as an expert who happens to bea phenomenal and articulate speaker on this specific topic. Then you are ready to take the next of three steps in turning your public speaking opportunities into a professional speaking career.

This now requires that you create an official website, email, internet presence that shows you are seriously in business, which includesyour speech title, an explanation of what makes you an expert on thistopic, and 'why they should listen to you,' with contact information for any meeting planner to find you and/or follow up with you after you have made your initial contact.

M 2: Market

Who needs your message? Who will be most benefitted? Who is in pain? Whom do you help? Which concepts, principles, laws, stories and data will you teach? Which sources do both you and your audience trust? How will you introduce it? How long will you speak? How will you conclude? What idea will your audience take home? Who would benefit from your message? Entrepreneurs, sales professionals, home-based business owners, military service men and women, emerging leaders, seasoned corporate executives, company managers, coaches, athletes, students, educators, administrators, trade association members?

This is your Market, who constitutes the specific people and organizations to whom you offer your extraordinary personal expertise.

M 3: Marketing

Where do the people and organizations that will benefit from your message gather for their meetings and trainings?

This becomes your Marketing focus and roadmap template that gives you a specific direction and an already scheduled timeline to follow.

With your Market now identified and your Marketing possibilities unveiled, you contact your local/city Chamber of Commerce (join them if necessary) and request a list of every company, trade association, and not-for-profit organization in your state, with their accompanying officers, job descriptions, revenues, vision, values, mission, reason for existing and favorite charity included in your information. Study the list and go after the 'low-hanging fruit' that have a conference or training coming up soon. Research the name of the decision-making meeting planner in the organization who hires the speakers and make an appointment to visit him/her in their office to explain exactly what, why, and how you and your unique and powerful message will be perfect for his/her next conference.

When he/she hires you, be extremely easy and professional to work with, and when you over deliver what you promised, you will make him/her the hero of the meeting, and look mighty good in front of their bosses!

You now take this great experience, which generated a magnificent flowery letter of recommendation from the CEO and/or meeting planner that you can market to other similar companies and organizations in your city, and especially to the other 49 state trade associations across America who will also benefit from your expertise, personality, passion and expertise. Voila! New business and referrals start to take care of themselves and you're up and running as a paid professional speaker.

Bottom line. By answering these three critical questions you have put yourself on a course of action that will be continuously fueled by the answers to three more reoccurring questions:

- What do I want the audience to learn or believe?
- What do I want to achieve personally from delivering this speech?
- How should I present the speech so they know I have more tosay and they should bring me back?

WHEN IT ALL COMES TOGETHER

A classic example of what can happen when all of these elements come together for a greater purpose to bless humanity with our talents and messages, is the transformational experience that began when I met an incredible human being.

In 2012 a young man named Anthony Robles, born with only one leg, won the National NCAA Wrestling Championship and was honored as the recipient of the Jimmy Valvano ESPY Award for Courage.

Anthony phoned me and asked if I would write his acceptance speech. I immediately flew into Phoenix, Arizona and interviewed him and his mother for 5+ hours where we Googled Jimmy Valvano to get an idea of who he was and why this prestigious award was named after him. The next few minutes would change both of our lives forever.

As a legendary NCAA basketball coach, Jimmy Valvano led his North Carolina State team to the National Championship in 1983. After fifteen years of coaching, he became a popular television sports commentator. Tragically, he was stricken with cancer, and his long battle came to an end a few weeks after he delivered his final speech at the inaugural ESPY Awards broadcast live on national television in 1993.

Standing at the podium with the light flashing in his face, signaling that he should stop talking, Valvano defiantly continued until he had delivered his last lecture and the message he wanted to leave the world. With tears in his eyes he simply said:

"To me, there are three things we all should do every day of our lives. Number one is laugh. You should laugh every day. Number two is think. You should spend some time in thought. Number three: you should have your emotions moved to tears— could be happiness or joy. Think about it. If you laugh, you think, and you cry, that's a full day. That's a heck of a day. You do that seven days a week, you're going to have something special." Coach Valvano concluded by saying, "Don't give up; don't ever give up."

Fast-forward to the 2012 ESPYA (Excellence in Sports Performance Yearly Award) as Anthony walked out on stage to a standing ovation from his fellow sports world superstars. With the world watching, he humbly honored his mother for never giving up on him even though she, a teenaged single mother, could have thought that raising a child with one leg was too much and could have given up Anthony for adoption. When Anthony was in college and she herself became ill and her husband walked out on the family and they lost their home she still didn't give up.

Anthony's mother stretched to care for him and encouraged him to stretch to pursue his dreams of wrestling. Anthony recognized that not everyone understands the power of stretch:

"At the beginning of my wrestling career, I lost most of my matches, and people said, 'It's okay. I'm proud of you for trying.' This ticked me off so bad! Losing is not okay! What they were really saying was that I was a handicapped kid and should be grateful that I could even participate."

Following his mother's example, he refused to settle, stretched to achieve his goals, and has now dedicated his life to inspiring others to stretch.

To express this dedication, Anthony Robles closed his ESPY acceptance speech by quoting a short poem I penned for the occasion that captures the essence of what Coach Valvano represented and what Anthony's inspirational story teaches the world.

Unstoppable

Every soul who comes to earth
With a leg or two at birth
Must wrestle his opponents knowing
It's not what is, it's what can be, that measures worth.
Make it hard, just make it possible
And through pain I'll not complain,
My spirit is unconquerable.
Fearless I will face each foe
For I know I am capable. Making winning personal
I don't care what's probable
Through blood, sweat, and tears,
I am Unstoppable!

(copyright Dan Clark 2012)

CHAPTER NINE

IS COMMUNICATION AN ART?

Logic, grammar, and rhetoric are the three arts that deal with excellence in the use of language for the expression of thought and feeling. Being grammatical and logical in our soliloquizing, while putting our thoughts and feelings down on paper, is all that is required and is often awarded with prestigious "Pulitzer Prizes." However, if we desire to be great and powerful public speakers, we must not merely have these two components in our presentation. To win a commitment to the conclusion and sentiment we proposed, we must fully embrace and use rhetoric.

The ancient and honorable art of rhetoric is the art of persuasion. To be an amazing public speaker requires both substance and style. Many take courses in public speaking, but most have not been trained in the skills of persuasion. The teaching of rhetoric has usually been about oration and style—style in the use of language and style that makes the communication of substance either more elegant or more effective in both the written and spoken word. However, it is critical to realize that elegance in weaving a tapestry of words may be a desired and mesmerizing bit of sizzle, but it will never compare in effectiveness and long-term impact with passionate persuasion.

The words *oratory* and *rhetoric* are not the same. Oratory is equated with the political platform, the courtroom, or the legislative assembly. Rhetoric is different, and for the definition we turn to the Greeks and Aristotle in his famous essay, "Rhetoric." Aristotle pointed out the three main tactics to be employed if one wished to succeed in the art of persuasion. The Greeks call these three instruments of persuasion Ethos, Pathos, and Logos.

ETHOS, PATHOS, LOGOS, MYTHOS

Ethos

Ethos signifies a person's character. Establishing your character is the preliminary step in any attempt at persuasion. Ethos means others listen to you because they sense that what you have to say is worth listening to. They sense you can be trusted for your honesty and good will and know what you are talking about. Of the three factors of persuasion, Ethos should always come first. Unless you have established your credibility as a speaker and made yourself attractive to your listeners, you will not sustain their attention, much less inspire them to do anything.

Pathos

Whereas Ethos consists in the establishment of the speaker's credibility and credentials (his or her respectable and admirable character), Pathos consists in arousing the passions of the listeners, getting their emotions running in the direction of the action to be taken. Pathos is the motivating factor.

Logos

Logos is the marshaling of reason and must come last. In speaking, it does you no good to give reasons and arguments until you have first established an emotional mood that is receptive to them. In other words, it is critical to first arouse favorable feelings toward your own person and feelings in favor of the end result you are seeking before you can reinforce the feelings with your list of whys. Reasons and arguments have no force unless your listeners are already disposed emotionally to move in the direction that your reasons justify.

All in all, Ethos epitomizes the reasons. Logos is the action to be taken by your listeners, and it confirms the feelings. Pathos is what you have already aroused. With Ethos and Pathos fully operative, Logos remains the winning trump card in the persuader's hand.

Mythos

An argument based on tradition, values of a group or identity that challenges the status quo in an even bold, politically incorrect way. Here is where you can deflect the controversial message to a third-party experience so it's not your opinion, you are simply reporting the facts.

CHAPTER TEN

THE ART OF COMMUNICATING

Communication is more than just two or more people taking turns talking. And it's definitely not thinking about what you are going to say next while waiting for the person who is currently talking to take a breath so that you can jump in with another of your "two cents." Steven Covey teaches "Seek first to understand, then to be understood." Communication is simply the clear understanding in a common language between two or more individuals.

A young mother was in her home talking on the phone. Somehow, her little four-year-old boy had managed to open the front door and wander out onto the sidewalk. As the mom looked out the window, she saw her son standing at the edge of their busy street with cars, trucks, and buses whipping by. Frantically, she dropped the phone, sprinted to the intersection, and picked him up just before he stepped out into oncoming traffic.

First hugging him and then holding him at arm's length, she scolded, "Johnny, how many times do I have to tell you, don't go near the curb!" With tears in his eyes, the frightened little guy replied, "Mommy, what's a curb?"

I once bought a parakeet and promptly started the arduous process of teaching it to talk. "Danny, Danny," I repeated over and over again— fifty repetitions a day for two straight months! I had given up when it finally happened. I was leaving the room and the parakeet blurted out, "Danny, Danny." Not one to stop at my first success, I decided to teach him his last name. "Clark, Clark," I said. This time it only took two hundred repetitions before the bird finally said, "Clark, Clark."

Then something very interesting happened. I got sick and spent two days in the house coughing. When I had recovered, I threw a party for some close friends. As I showed off my talking bird, I discovered a great principle about the education process. I put the bird on my finger and, with a little prompting, it said, "Danny Clark." Then, to everyone's amusement, the bird coughed. Of course I didn't teach the bird to cough; he had picked it up the two days I was sick. But it did prove that even a bird is a product of its environment. So are human beings. What goes into our minds will eventually come out.

If you grew up with some bad habits, don't be upset at the people who raised you. Just learn this lesson: if you are one way, you can change. You can be different. You can be any which way you want. Just alter your negative environment and hang in there until you get the desired result. Remember, it's not what's on the outside that matters. Birds communicate with birds, dogs with dogs, people with people, and, most interesting to me, people with birds and dogs and circus elephants and lions and tigers! The Horse Whisperer communicates with horses, and the trainers at Sea World communicate with dolphins and the killer whale Shamu!

Verbal and nonverbal signs, signals, sounds, body language, voice inflections, eye contact, and hand gestures—they are all forms of communication. Humans even have a deeper form of communicating I call the Language of the Heart. I wrote about it in one of my songs:

Language of the Heart

There's a secret language only lovers know
Following their hearts to places heads can never go
Without a word, their lips and hands and want-me-eyes reveal
Like dancing partners sensing where to go, they move by feel

Yes, the eyes are the window to the soul
Lovers look inside and see that passion makes them whole
Lustfully they fantasize about how love should be
Then find a soul mate seeking self-fulfilling prophecy

Language of the heart is never said or written down
Words can't capture what we mean, the silence makes the sound
Spirit talks to spirit through emotions set apart
The language only lovers know, the language of the heart

There's a secret language only lovers know
Feeling, self-revealing, laying low, and goin' slow
Hearing, tasting, smelling, touching, seeing senses flow
Body talk connecting, only honesty can show

A squeezing one, two, three says I love you
A nod and sultry smile says I am thinking 'bout you, too
Touching toes beneath the table is better than dessert
And without public affection is the way real lovers flirt

A tender touch says more than words can say
A kiss heals hurt and sends the pain away
Holding me, like you'll never let me go
Is the reason why I know...

THE POWER OF QUESTIONS

When you analyze our communication, you will realize that you cannot 'not' answer a question. Are you a conservative republican or a liberal Democrat, or Independent? Are you tall, short, male, female, spiritual, fast, slow, etc., etc.? For this reason, the quickest way to engage an audience is to ask them a question. At the end of the day (at by the end of your speech) everyone will realize that life is not about the answers. It's about the questions. We can't just focus on answering the questions – we must question the answers! The following is my favorite story about the significance of questions:

A college professor asked his students to list what they thought were the Seven Wonders of the World. Out of the hundred students in the lecture hall, the general consensus was:

1. Egypt's pyramids
2. Great Wall of China
3. Grand Canyon
4. Taj Mahal
5. Rainbow Bridge
6. Niagara Falls
7. St. Peter's Basilica

While gathering the votes, the professor noted that one girl had not yet finished her paper. He asked if she was having trouble answering the question. She replied, "No, I'm not having trouble with the answer, I'm having trouble with the question.

"Why only seven? According to whom and what criteria? What does 'wonder' mean to you, and is it different for me?"

The professor responded, "Tell us what you have, and maybe we can help."

The girl hesitated and then read, "I think the real Seven Wonders of the World are: to see, to hear, to taste, to touch, to laugh, to feel, and to love."

The room was so quiet you could have heard a pin drop.

The professor took a deep breath and replied, "Wow! This is the most profound lesson we will learn all year. And isn't it pathetic that out of the 101 people in this room – me included – that only one of us, only 1 percent, understands that the things we overlook as simple and fundamental truly are wondrous?"

This story provides three powerful reminders:

- The most important and precious things in life cannot be bought or built by hand.
- Before we look for answers outside of ourselves, let us first look within.
- Life is not about answers; it's about questions.

ASKING THE 'RIGHT' QUESTIONS

Questioning is the most common method of influence used by master persuaders. Skilled negotiators ask more than twice as many questions as average negotiators. As public speakers, the quickest way to engage an audience is to ask a compelling question.

Questions elicit an automatic response from our brains. Even if we don't verbalize an answer, we think of a response every time we are asked a question.

This means life is not about answers it's a string of back-to-back questions linked together, fueled by our curiosity and commitment to uncover the whole truth. This also means that the person who asks the questions controls the conversation, knowing you can get wrong answers from negative questions and you can get wrong answers from right questions, but you cannot get right answers from wrong questions. Only when we ask the right questions can we get the right answers and progress to the next right question.

Questions beginning with "why" and "who" are more emotionally charged than "what" or "how" questions because "why" and "who" questions are historical in nature. They take us back in time. "Why did this happen?" "Why must you drive drunk now?" "Who messed up?" They plead for reasons, but they breed excuses. We all despise excuses and get annoyed when others use them on us, but the fault is usually with those asking the wrong "why" and "who" questions. They are simply answering the question we asked.

"WHY" AND "WHO" QUESTIONS ARE REGRESSIVE, FOCUSED ON HISTORY AND EMOTIONALLY KEEP US STUCK IN THE PAST.

"WHAT" AND "HOW" QUESTIONS ARE PROGRESSIVE, FOCUSED ON THE PRESENT AND LOGICALLY KEEP US MOVING TOWARD THE FUTURE.

Instead of asking people to live in the past, we should ask future-oriented questions like "How can we fix this?" or "What can we do right now to stop the decline and turn this around?"

When a speaker asks the right questions, not only does he/she immediately turn the audience into listeners, but he/she accelerates the answers to the three Speaker Triangle questions: Why Should I Listen To You? Can I Do It Too? How Do I Do It?

THE POWER OF HUMOR

Stereotypically, public speakers should avoid talking about religion and politics; however, when tastefully done, a true pro can mix the two to establish him or herself as a bold, straightforward speaker. One of my favorite examples is: President Bush and his secret service are walking through a building when they see an old man with a beard and walking stick, wearing a robe and sandals. President Bush immediately sends over one of his men to speak to the man. "Excuse me, President Bush wants to know if you're Moses." The old man lowers his head and doesn't say a word. Again, the agent asks, "Sir, the president wants to know if you are Moses." Again, the old man says nothing.

Frustrated, President Bush walks over himself and asks, "Are you Moses?" This time, the old man turns his back and walks away. President Bush and his entourage storm off. Seeing what happened, a curious bystander approaches the old man and asks the same question, "Are you Moses?" This time the old man answers, "Yes, I am." The bystander asks, "Then why didn't you acknowledge that to the president?" Moses answers, "Because the last time I talked to a bush, I ended up wandering in the wilderness for forty years and leading my people to the only place in the Middle East that doesn't have any oil!"

THE POWER OF WORDS

As in "Paint A Colorful Word Picture."

The reason you write out your story in a first iteration is so you can go back in the editing process to create a second version where, "every word pays its own way," and you eliminate the redundancies. This is also when you begin the process of replacing your regular, mundane, ordinary verbs with action verbs that paint a colorful and textured "word picture" that makes your character or the scene come alive. The following is a continuous scenario that should inspire you to become a "wordsmith" by choosing stimulating words to describe the mundane:

- If you "led" a company project from start to finish, replace it with: Chaired, Orchestrated.

- If you actually "developed" and "introduced" that project into your company, use: Founded, Engineered, Formulated, Launched, Pioneered, Spearheaded.

- If you helped your team operate more efficiently and "saved" money replace this weak word with: Deducted, Diagnosed, Reconciled, Yielded.

- If your work "increased" the company's numbers and profitability use electrifying verbs like: Accelerated, Amplified, Boosted, Capitalized, Maximized, Outpaced, Stimulated.

- Because you led the company "conversion" from an analog operating system to digital use the descriptors: Customized, Modified, Overhauled, Rehabilitated, Remodeled, Revamped, Revitalized, Streamlined, Transformed.

- Instead of "leading a team" or "managing employees" use terms like: Coached, Aligned, Cultivated, Fostered, Mobilized, Shaped, Unified.

- Because you were "responsible for" a great new partner, sponsor, or source of funding use: Forged, Navigated, Partnered, Secured.

- Because "customer service" is not a department, but a way of life, your job of answering questions and overcoming objections should be described as one who has: Advocated, Arbitrated, Fielded, Dispatched, Monitored, Screened, Scrutinized.

- A coworker whose job it is to "research" and "analyze" will feel more significant when you describe what they do as: Audited, Calculated, Explored, Forecasted, Mapped, Qualified, Quantified, Tracked.

- When asked to "describe" and "explain" what you learned in a training meeting with a coworker, tell them you were: Briefed, Counseled, Critiqued, and Coaxed so you would Campaign what they Composed.

- When you "hit" your goals, "reach" your sales quota and "win" a coveted department award, describe your accomplishments using: Outperformed, Showcased, Surpassed, Targeted

CHAPTER ELEVEN

WHY SHOULD WE TELL STORIES?

"A need to tell and hear stories is essential to the species Homo sapiens – second in necessity apparently after nourishment and before love and shelter. Millions survive without love or home, almost none in silence; the opposite of silence leads quickly to narrative, and the sound of story is the dominant sound of our lives, from the small accounts of our day's events to the vast incommunicable constructs of psychopaths." —Reynolds Price

Life is not about answers. It's about asking the right questions. Therefore, when it comes to figuring out why we all should tell stories, perhaps the better questions are:

- Why do human beings laugh and do what is necessary to laugh again and again?
- Why do we cry and always feel better after we do?
- Why are human beings so obsessed with purpose?
- What evolutionary purpose do humans serve?
- Why are we inherently social beings who search for our tribe and seek out 'our' people?
- Why is the most powerful motivator to overcome our fears and doubts always a story about someone who has done what we are afraid and need to do?

The answers are not many, but only one: life is a story that connects our mind with our heart, and our senses to our purpose. In other words, a story – our individual stories – help us find our personal 'why,' which leads us through the process of identifying and executing our what, converting our needs into wants, with an urgent when, and a clear how.

My friend and colleague Patricia Fripp, a Hall of Fame speaker and extraordinary speech coach, reminds us that more than any words you say in your presentation, your audience will remember what they "see" in their minds while they are listening. Everybody loves a good story. No matter our culture, we grow up feeling that hearing a story is somehow a reward. Stories are the best way to explain the complex, motivate, and train. The art of storytelling is essential to effective public speaking.

By definition, storytelling is the conveying of events in words, sound and/or images, often by improvisation or embellishment. Stories or narratives have been shared in every culture as a means of entertainment, education, cultural preservation and instilling moral values. Crucial elements of stories and storytelling include plot, characters and narrative point of view. The term 'storytelling' is used in a narrow sense to refer specifically to oral storytelling and also in a looser sense to refer to techniques used in other media to unfold or disclose the narrative of a story.

Storytelling is one of the oldest forms of communication, before writing and even drawing on cave walls. Since humans are social beings, stories communicated things, and explained things that made no logical sense to early tribes. Storytelling allowed history and culture to be passed from generation to generation and gave people a sense of belonging to their unique society.

As far back as we have written records there have been stories written down. It is very easy for me to imagine our ancestors prior to the written word sitting around the fire in the evening listening to a talented storyteller. The oldest written stories we have are clay tablets written in cuneiform over four thousand years ago. Some of these seem to be the precursors of some of the bible stories. Later about 2500 years ago there are stories written by the early Greeks; Homer's epic poems of heroes and demigods; the plays of Euripides,

Sophocles and Aristophanes, etc. I could go on and on throughout history and list innumerable great stories and storytellers. Some are histories, some are moral tales, some are epic adventures and some are merely entertainment.

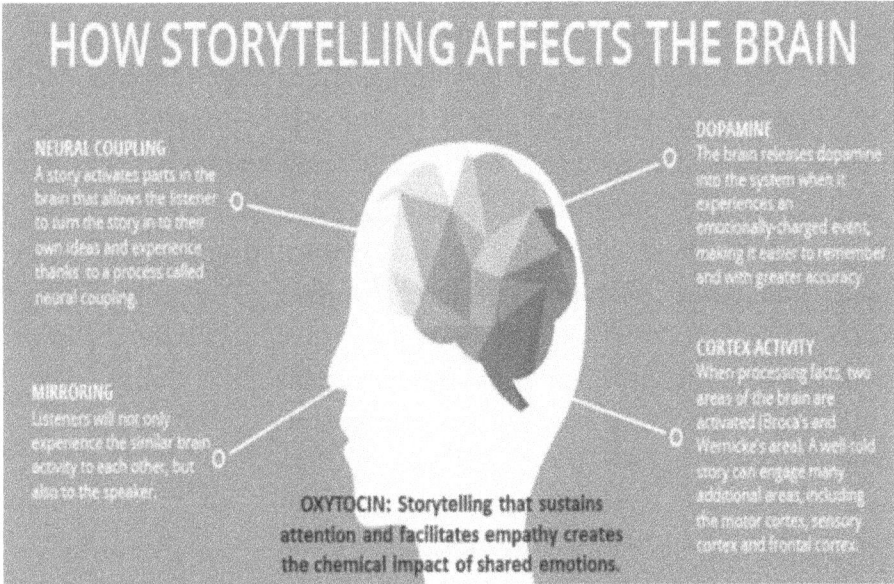

HOW STORYTELLING AFFECTS THE BRAIN

NEURAL COUPLING
A story activates parts in the brain that allows the listener to turn the story in to their own ideas and experience thanks to a process called neural coupling.

MIRRORING
Listeners will not only experience the similar brain activity to each other, but also to the speaker.

DOPAMINE
The brain releases dopamine into the system when it experiences an emotionally-charged event, making it easier to remember and with greater accuracy.

CORTEX ACTIVITY
When processing facts, two areas of the brain are activated (Broca's and Wernicke's area). A well-told story can engage many additional areas, including the motor cortex, sensory cortex and frontal cortex.

OXYTOCIN: Storytelling that sustains attention and facilitates empathy creates the chemical impact of shared emotions.

Humans have an inherent readiness or predisposition to organize experience into story form: into viewpoints, characters, intentions, sequential plot structures and the rest (Bruner).

100,000 years of evolutionary reliance on story has built into the human genetic code instructions to wire the brain to think in terms of stories from birth (Pinker).

It is because of the narrative nature of human minds at and before birth that we are impelled as adults to make sense of our lives in terms of narrative (McAdams).

THE SCIENCE OF STORYTELLING

Why Telling a Story Is the Most Powerful Way to Activate Our Brains and Connect with Others

(Research By Leo Widrich)

A good story can make or break a presentation, article, or conversation. But why is that? When *the researcher and writer of this article* started to market his product through stories instead of benefits and bullet points, sign-ups went through the roof. The answer is revealed in the following historic tale, followed by the simple science behind why storytelling is so uniquely powerful.

In 1748, the British politician and aristocrat John Montagu, the 4th Earl of Sandwich, spent a lot of his free time playing cards. He greatly enjoyed eating a snack while still keeping one hand free for the cards. So he came up with the idea to eat beef between slices of toast, which would allow him to finally eat and play cards at the same time. Eating his newly invented "sandwich," the name for two slices of bread with meat in between, became one of the most popular meal inventions in the western world.

What's interesting about this is that you are very likely to never forget the story of who invented the sandwich ever again. Or, at least, much less likely to do so if it had been presented to us in bullet points or another purely information-based form. For over 27,000 years, since the first cave paintings were discovered, telling stories has been one of our most fundamental communication methods.

OUR BRAIN ON STORIES

We all enjoy a good story, whether it's a novel, a movie, or simply something one of our friends is explaining to us. But why do we feel so much more engaged when we hear a narrative about events?

It's quite simple. If we listen to a PowerPoint presentation with boring bullet points, a certain part in the brain gets activated. Scientists call this Broca's area and Wernicke's area. Overall, it hits our language processing parts in the brain, where we decode words into meaning. And that's it. Nothing else happens.

When we are being told a story, things change dramatically. Not only are the language processing parts in our brain activated, but any other area in our brain that we would use when experiencing the events of the story are too.

If someone tells us about how delicious certain foods were, our sensory cortex lights up. If it's about motion, our motor cortex gets active: "Metaphors like 'The singer had a velvet voice' and 'He had leathery hands' roused the sensory cortex. Then, the brains of participants were scanned as they read sentences like 'John grasped the object' and 'Pablo kicked the ball.' The scans revealed activity in the motor cortex, which coordinates the body's movements."

A story can put your whole brain to work. And, yet, it gets better: When we tell others stories that have really helped us shape our thinking and way of life, we can have the same effect on them, too. The brains of the person telling a story and listening to it can synchronize.

Evolution has wired our brains for storytelling – how to make use of it. Now all this is interesting. We know that we can activate our brains better if we listen to stories. The still unanswered question is: Why is that? Why does the format of a story, where events unfold one after the other, have such a profound impact on our learning?

The simple answer is this: We are wired that way. A story, if broken down into the simplest form, is a connection of cause and effect. And that is exactly how we think. We think in narratives all day long, no matter if it is about buying groceries, whether we think about work or our spouse at home. We make up (short) stories in our heads for every action and conversation. In fact, Jeremy Hsu found that, "personal stories and gossip make up 65% of our conversations."

Whenever we hear a story, we want to relate it to one of our existing experiences. That's why metaphors work so well with us. While we are busy searching for a similar experience in our brains, we activate a part called 'insula,' which helps us relate to that same experience of pain, joy, or disgust.

We link up metaphors and literal happenings automatically. Everything in our brain is looking for the cause and effect relationship of something we've previously experienced. The next time you struggle with getting people on board with your projects and ideas, simply tell them a story, where the outcome is that doing what you had in mind is the best thing to do. According to Princeton researcher Hasson, storytelling is the only way to plant ideas into other people's minds.

CHAPTER TWELVE

IS THERE AN ART TO REVEALING, WRITING, AND PRESENTING YOUR 'SIGNATURE STORY'?

A "Signature Story" is something everybody has. It is based on an understanding of what psychologists call, "SEE" experiences, or Significant Emotional Events.

A Significant Emotional Event is something that happened to you, where you can quantify exactly how you thought and behaved BEFORE it occurred, and how you now think and behave differently BECAUSE it occurred. These could include your marriage, the birth of your firstborn child, dealing with and/or overcoming a serious illness, the death of a loved one, a devastating divorce, being laid off at work, graduating from college, getting an exciting job promotion, and anything else that causes Post Traumatic Stress, where we can't stop remembering.

Once we have identified this magnanimous event, we must revisit the emotion of the victory or defeat, and relive the pleasure or pain that the event caused us. We find a quiet, secluded spot away from the distractions of the world where we can begin the deep meditation process of examining this experience from every possible angle to find the nuggets of wisdom, pillars of profound understanding, rays of light, and life-altering lessons that we learned from it.

On a personal note, let me share two of my "Significant Emotional Events" – one that changed my perspective on living; the other that changed the course of my life – both of which I have turned into my "signature stories."

The first version of your Signature Story is the bare-naked, unadulterated, facts only, non-emotional description of exactly what happened, with no embellishment or explanation of what you learned from it.

SOARING TO THE EDGE OF SPACE

A few years ago, on October 23, 2010, I had the opportunity to fly in a U2 Spy Plane where for five hours I got to see the curvature of the earth. It changed my perspective on life forever!" That's it.

ANOTHER "SEE"

The second "Significant Emotional Event" that changed me and my life forever occurred on an American football field. One day during my American football practice session, the coach whistled, "go," and another player and I ran full speed into each other to practice our tackling technique.

After the brutal head-on collision I lay on the ground in shock, with a sharp, piercing pain shooting through my body. My eye drooped and my speech slurred (which momentarily returned), my right side went numb and my right arm dangled helplessly at my side. By nightfall my neck was stiff. I perspired profusely, shook, and threw up until I cried myself to sleep. For the next fourteen months I was paralyzed—both physically and emotionally. I went to sixteen different doctors, fifteen of whom told me I would not recover – I would not get any better. However, over the course of six months of self-invented physical therapy I fought my way back to a 95% recovery.

UNVEILING YOUR SIGNIFICANT EMOTIONAL EVENTS

It's now time for you to go back in your life and conduct a self-audit of good and bad, superficial and deeply moving experiences that will help you recall and illuminate your "Significant Emotion Events." After you make a list of as many life-changing events that you can remember, evaluate which one actually changed you in the most dramatic way – physically, mentally, spiritually, emotionally, socially, in your family and/or your commitment to humanitarian charity.

Once you have singled out this specific event as the "mother of all emotional events" in your life, continue the searching, pondering, evaluating process of figuring out what life lessons you learned from it that are worth sharing with someone else.

After you have your list of the things you learned from this event, it is time to turn this experience into your "Signature Story."

THE EMBELLISHMENT PROCESS OF WRITING YOUR SIGNATURE STORY

The bare-bones report of my adventure into space is boring and non-eventful, eh? It is through the 'embellishment process' that you make the story come alive with words like 'soar' and phrases like 'sitting in the sounds of silence.'

The Embellished version full of 'word pictures and philosophy and wonderment:

On October 23, I had the rare opportunity to soar to the edge of space in a U2 Reconnaissance Aircraft: (YouTubedanclarku2spyplane).

Because it was a classified mission, I can only tell you that at 70,000 feet you can see two-thirds of the state of California. At 80,000 feet you see mapped outlines of America. And at 90,000 feet

(17 miles) you tear up and realize that if mortality is all there is, what a waste this life will be! In a sortie that lasted five hours, I sat in the sounds of silence, looking at the breathtaking curvature of the earth, gazing into the endless eternity of space where I could see the blue atmosphere turn to black, experiencing an unobstructed view of the universe, and with a seventeen-mile-high perspective on life and leadership, I realized that we are all interconnected in a world governed by a specific set of universal laws.

Alone with my thoughts, I pondered, "Could we be more than mere mortal beings, living on a small planet, for a short season?" When we landed, I realized everything we can take with us when we die, I had aboard with me on that aircraft: my education, my character, my convictions, and my memory whether or not I left a legacy of leadership, service before self, and unconditional love behind that validated my life mattered.

So... what do you think? Are these two 'Significant Emotional Events' inspirational? Are there any life lessons that I learned that are worthy of sharing with others? Could these experiences be entertaining, educational, thought provoking, and serve as a call-to-action with take-home value?

The only way to find out is if you write down the event and then begin the process of 'Story Boarding,' which is the "Process of Embellishment."

The dictionary definition of *embellishment* is "an elaboration, decorative and enhanced detail or feature added to something to make it more attractive, interesting and entertaining."

Knowing my bottom-line story, the following is my "Signature Story" in its entirety so you can read it and compare/contrast where and when and how I "embellished" it with decorative jokes, entertaining one-liners, quotable quotes, and interesting philosophical lessons learned.

Remember, when writing your "Embellished Signature Story" you included every detail, so when you begin the "Editing Process" where you cut away the irrelevant clutter and boring details, you will know what to leave in your final version.

DAN'S "SIGNATURE STORY"

I played American football for thirteen years, until the first day of practice in my last season, when my lifelong dream of playing professional football and baseball was taken away.

In a tackling drill, two of us ran into each other at full speed. From fifteen yards apart my teammate's helmet violently crashed into my helmet, my right shoulder was smashed into the cutting edge of my fiberglass pads, and we slammed to the ground, momentarily knocking me unconscious. When Lyle got off of me, my eye drooped, my speech was slurred, my right side was pierced with the penetrating pain that felt like my body was on fire. My right arm dangled helplessly at my side.

The medical report would show that my momentary eye and speech conditions resulted from a severe blow to the head when I slammed to the ground, giving me a level two concussion where the blood vessels in my brain were stretched, and cranial nerves may have been damaged. My sight and speech returned to normal within seconds. However, I had compressed my seventh cervical vertebrae (which doctors didn't discover until months later because they presupposed, I had only injured my shoulder), and severed the axillary nerve in my right deltoid, which left my shoulder function useless. All this in one hit, in one moment in time.

The pain was so weird and devastating that the only way I can describe it is that I felt like I had hit my crazy bone in my elbow – except that the intense burning and tingling ripped through my entire right side from my head to my toes and then went numb.

I handled the day okay, but unbearable pain hit me that night in bed. I shook like a leaf, profusely perspired, and threw up, crying myself to sleep in a pool of self-pity and denial. The details are mostly irrelevant, so let me simply connect the dots.

At this time, there was limited research and understanding about concussions, not realizing that sometimes it takes months or years for to fully heal. Add to that my complications. I spent time with Los Angeles team physician Dr. Frank Jobe, the world-famous orthopedic genius, at Centinela Hospital in Inglewood, California. He treated patients from all over the world and in 1974 had performed reconstructive surgery on Los Angeles Dodger pitcher Tommy John, with the operation being chronicled in a five-page expose in Sports Illustrated.

I also underwent tests and therapy at Craig Rehabilitation Center in Denver, Colorado. I remained numb for fourteen months and went to sixteen doctors, fifteen of whom projected that my arm would always dangle at my side, telling me I would never get any better.

Have you ever heard this? What happens if you believe it? You never get any better.

Sure it was a physical injury, but it affected my whole life. I was an athlete and got a lot of attention because of it. I was somebody because I played football and baseball and enjoyed free food at restaurants, status at celebrity galas, fame and glory. I was going to be an overpaid NFL superstar. But in a single moment, a freak accident took away my identity. Suddenly I was nobody to my coaches and nobody to my teammates and fans. Even more devastating, I became nobody to myself.

Have you ever lost your identity or at some point seriously questioned who you really are? Before you can like or love someone else, you first must like and love yourself. To like and love requires that you know and understand. I was lost, lonely, and confused.

I couldn't write—I was right-handed. I couldn't concentrate on work or education because it constantly felt like some wild animal was biting my neck and shoulder.

I used to get electrical, shocking nerve impulses in my shoulder that would shake my arm like it was plugged into a light socket. This made me afraid to go out in public, especially on a date, because my arm might blast her in the chops. One time I was sitting with my family at dinner when my arm flipped out and knocked a bowl of mayonnaise off the table. The next morning my younger brother showed up to breakfast wearing goggles and a batting helmet!

Needless to say I hit rock bottom, and life as I knew it was nowhere to be found. I didn't know if I even wanted to live. Have you ever felt like that? Have you ever been so down and confused that you thought you should leave your family, isolate yourself from friends, and contemplate checking-out altogether? Before long I fell into what I thought was deep depression and suicidal ideology.

TWO PRESSING QUESTIONS

Question #1: "Why would I want to give up and quit everything?"

The first reason I gave up and decided to quit was because I had confused who I was with what I did. Have any of you? I thought being an athlete was who I was, when in reality it was only what I did. Have any of you ever confused the difference between the person and the performance? Turns out that playing football and baseball was what I did, not who I was as a man. And when we identify ourselves in terms of what we do instead of who we are, we become human doings instead of human beings – unacceptable, if lasting happiness and a life of significance is truly what we seek.

Sounds good and simple, right? However, shifting my priorities was the hardest thing I've ever had to do! In one moment, I was faced with the emotional pain of giving up my life's dream and the identity I had grown up with. Outside, I was an athlete. Inside, I knew it was time to find a new game.

The second reason I gave up and decided to quit was because I thought I was depressed. I was not just paralyzed physically – I was also paralyzed emotionally! And what happens when you think you are depressed? You are depressed. Without raising your hands, does anyone here think they are depressed?

With all due respect, I realize there are people here and friends and loved ones we know who have been diagnosed with a chemical imbalance, who need medication, and non-judgmental friendships and unconditional love. They suffer from depression and we are there for them!

However, through my experience I also know getting better mentally and emotionally was a prerequisite to recovering physically. My improvement began when I realized there is a huge difference between being depressed and being disappointed – a giant difference between being depressed and being discouraged. When you are disappointed and discouraged you don't need medication that flatlines your emotions and dries out your human spirit to fight and survive!

Psychologists remind us to be on guard of H.A.L.T.S. – which is avoiding being Hungry, Angry, Lonely, Tired and Sad – all of which distort our ability to think clearly and drain our energy to stay motivated. When I was injured I didn't suddenly have a chemical imbalance and need medication. What I needed was a change in attitude and perspective to focus on identifying my why so I could again make winning personal!

Yes, I had some caring loved ones and associates come up to me and say, "I'm sorry and know what you are going through." But no they did not! No one does. Psychologists teach us that the average person talks between 100 and 200 words per minute, and yet we think between 200 and 400 words per minute – which means no one ever really knows everything we think or feel or want to say. The author Thoreau wrote, "Men lead lives of quiet desperation."

So what do we do? To whom do we turn? Luckily, I had some loyal friends and family members who stuck by me who continuously reminded me, "You can't quit – it's a league rule;" "No matter what your past has been you have a spotless future;" "We can't always control what happens, but we can always control what happens next!"

What I needed to begin my recovery was to start dreaming again and set some realistic goals that would keep me from letting what I could not do, interfere with what I still could do.

The third reason I stayed paralyzed for fourteen months was because I was asking the wrong questions. I was asking the doctors, "How to get better?" when I should have been asking myself, "Why should I get better?" You see, once we answer and identify "why," figuring out the "how-to" is simple. Not easy. If it were easy everybody would do it. Learning to do hard things is what makes life significant, and is what turns a boy into a man and a girl into a woman, and a manager into a leader.

Question #2: "Why didn't I quit?"

Bottom line. My why became bigger than my 'why not.' In addition to my small group of true friends who kept me laughing and never allowed my to feel sorry for myself, there were four people who triggered a combination of outside-in inspiration and inside-out resolve, who helped keep me focused for another six months of rehab, pushing me to relentlessly work hard and persevere until I recovered.

First, I had a doctor, the sixteenth specialist – Dr. Brent Pratley – an extraordinary orthopedic surgeon who was on the cutting edge of technology and techniques. He gave me the scientific hope, made me laugh and cope, and brought out my passion and imagination to do whatever I could think of that would help me get better.

WHEN MY RECOVERY BEGAN

Second, I had another doctor, Craig Buhler – a chiropractor by training – introduce me to his unique and powerful Advanced Muscle Integration Technique (AMIT) – which is a systematic treatment of joint and muscle conditions that has revolutionized preventative and rehabilitative sports medicine. Craig is a gifted healer who reminded me that doctors don't heal anybody – they just surgically repair when needed, and/or trigger systems already inside of us to help us heal ourselves. My body did not respond to the physical therapy and my nerves didn't begin to regenerate until I started seeing Craig on a weekly basis for treatments, while he schooled me in the significance of 'holistic medicine,' natural remedies and organic nutrition.

Third, I was given some counsel by an ecclesiastical leader who reminded me of the practical application of the law of the harvest: when you plant wheat you get wheat; when you plant expectations, purpose, hard work and clear consequences you get desired results. You don't reap what you deserve – you reap what you sow.

The fourth person who kept me focused was University of Utah Vice President Normand Gibbons. In my despair, he shared with me Sigmund Freud's famous paper on his 'Four Premises: All power is in the subconscious and lurks inside; We cannot investigate it by ourselves and alone: It's a mess down there; The pain in the subconscious is the cause of our failures.'

Dr. Gibbons also shared Freud's solution to combat these Premises that he calls 'Sublimation.' It suggests that instead of negatively reacting to pain, anger, frustration, and disappointment and allowing them to get us down and hold us back, we should positively respond and use them as fuel to test our resolve, overcome each obstacle, and prove every naysayer wrong. In other words, pain is the secret to achievement.

Dr. Gibbons then gave me a recording of a speech given by internationally renowned motivational teacher named Zig Ziglar, who soon would become a personal friend and my sponsor into the National Speakers Association in 1982. I had never heard of Zig and thought his mom had run out of names!

Out of curiosity I listened to his 45-minute speech, which through the use of humor and inspirational stories kick-started my inside-out recovery. In his rhythmic southern drawl, Zig spoke directly to me through one specific story:

"A struggling oilman in Texas, in his last-ditch effort to strike it rich, drilled one more time and hit a giant oil reserve so big that it gushed from the ground with such force that it literally destroyed the derrick. In an instant, the man became a millionaire. Or did he? Had not the oil always been down there? He had always been a millionaire but just didn't know it? All he had to do was dig down deeper and get out what was already there and use it for what it was meant to be used." Can you see why this one tale meant so much to me, and how it inspired me to coin five phrases that have served as a source of motivation to me and others ever since:

We don't see things as they are – we see things as we are. You get the man right and the world is right.

Things happen for a reason. But it is our responsibility to determine what that reason is.

Adversity introduces us to ourselves – no one can ever know how strong we are until we are stretched and tested.

Pain is a signal to grow, not to suffer. Once we learn the lesson the pain is teaching us, the pain goes away. Which means in life there are no mistakes, only lessons.

Crisis does not make or break a person – it just reveals the true character within.

Zig's story pierced my mind and heart to look inside myself and hang tough long enough to drill down deep enough to discover the untapped reserve of passion, purpose, and perseverance that was stuck beneath my surface just waiting to be used.

I started getting better physically *and* emotionally only when I started focusing on purposes instead of just setting goals. I stopped focusing on having fame and started focusing on being whole. I discovered that in order to get a better answer you've got to ask a better question, and as I previously mentioned: the question I asked of each of the sixteen doctors —"How do I get better?"— was not the right question. The better question was not to the doctors, but to myself:

"*Why*?" which generated a conclusion that: "Whatever it takes, I will endure to the end because this is what I am going to do *when* I get better."

Focusing on how to get better had set me up for failure because each doctor had a different theory, and the pain was so excruciating that quitting before fully recovering would have been easy and reasonable.

However, because of the influences I've shared and the emotional healing I first experienced, I fought back physically, mentally, and spiritually to a 95 percent recovery. All the feeling returned to my right side except in my right shoulder, which has remained totally numb. The nerves never regenerated. We must have nerve impulse and action to keep a muscle strong or, as in my case, it atrophies.

Yes, I went to the Raiders' training camp. But I never made my dream of becoming an NFL superstar come true. However, because of my career as a professional speaker and my studies to become an expert in managing change, building teams, and taking personal and organizational productivity to the next level, I have stayed involved in the NFL, and have branched out into the NCAA, NBA, and the PGA, working with teams and individual players and Fortune 500 executives and employees, and military and educational leaders on personal leadership that makes each of them an important ingredient in creating a winning organization.

MY CONCLUSION?

This football injury is clearly one of the best things that has ever happened to me. Don't misunderstand. My paralyzing accident isn't one of the best things that has happened to me – but what I learned about life and priorities and who I have become as a man as a result of going through this setback, makes it one of the best things that has ever happened to me. I now know that when you identify your 'why' and it becomes bigger than your 'why not,' you make winning personal and definitely discover 'how' to turn every stumbling block into a steppingstone, and every setback into a comeback!

BOTTOM LINE EVALUATION

As I previously mentioned, this experience is way too long to share in a speech and must be edited down so "Every Word Pays Its Own Way" by eliminating all of the detail that may be important to me, but that is definitely not important to the audience or relevant in conveying my message.

However, it is only a success story until I dive deeper to uncover the numerous messages it reveals. Embellishing it with quotes, humor and life lessons is what makes it come alive and become my 'signature story.'

THE SCIENCE OF
PUBLIC
SPEAKING

CHAPTER THIRTEEN

WHAT IS THE SCIENCE BEHIND CRAFTING A SPEECH LISTENER'S LOVE?

The Six Steps to Crafting a Powerful Memorable Speech: Shhh! Huh? Why? How? Where? When?

SHHH

The speaker is being introduced. *Wow! Listen to this.* Shhh, *this guy sounds like he will be amazing.* Your formal introduction should be viewed as part of your speech. It should be typed, double-spaced, fourteen-point bold font, no italics, printed on your letterhead, and physically handed to the person who is going to introduce you. Most likely they have already retrieved it from your website and have included it in their master copy script for your meeting session, but this is your tactful way to make sure the organization has not taken editorial liberties and changed it.

Don't ever trust anyone else to write your introduction from your bio or a book cover. The reason you physically give a copy of your introduction to the introducer is so you can meet them and they can feel your positive energy and get excited about having you as their speaker. It also gives you the chance to tell them your introduction is part of your speech, and, therefore, they should read it verbatim. Your introduction should never be longer than sixty seconds. The longer the introduction, the more insecure the speaker! The introduction serves one purpose—to build your credibility, expose your character, and answer for each audience member the question: Why should I listen to him?

HUH?

Speaker coach Max Dixon says, "Primitive brain scans for threat. People don't buy because they understand. They buy because they are understood. Consequently, the quickest way to build authenticity and connect with the audience is to smile. When we first see you, does your behavior inspire trust and turn your attendees into listeners? To the degree this relates to likability, the most significant ingredient is the face."

The smile is the first impression and the ice breaker, followed by eye contact with many individuals, one at a time, on several different rows, which clearly sends the message that you're personable, approachable, nowhere else but there, and that yes, you do understand. Remember that your "home onstage" is in the faces in your audience. Finding a friendly face fast is a confidence builder, but the goal is to connect with everybody. The face will usually be the dominant thermometer of whether you are hot or cold with the crowd and the level of your rapport and connection.

In sports we know that momentum is only as good as your next play. With the momentum now created by your concise, credibility-building introduction, the most important part of your speech is the first sixty seconds. I call it "Huh?" because that's what so many of us say when we are startled out of our sleep. "Huh?" symbolizes that when we step onstage, everybody is tired and nobody wants to be in this meeting. They would rather be outside doing something fun. Why on earth would anyone make them sit there and listen to another boring lecture?

"Huh?" is the "Okay, you woke me up with the fascinating introduction, so this better be good! You've got my attention, now keep it!" For this reason, if we are given a topic to speak on such as drinking and driving, you never start your speech by saying, "I've been asked to speak on drinking and driving." This is boring, gets no one's attention, and is a typical beginning for every amateur. Your first sixty seconds is the most important part. As the saying goes, you never get a second chance to make a first impression, so a better attention-getting technique is expected and required, such as, "One hundred thirteen teenagers were killed this weekend." If your assigned topic is wearing seat belts, you don't begin by saying, "I've been assigned to talk to you about the importance of wearing your seat belt."

A better "Huh?" attention getter is a shocker like, "A friend of mine, who is the proud father of nine children, killed his two youngest daughters last Wednesday." I guarantee in both of these examples every audience member immediately becomes a listener!

WHY?

Why did you bring this up? How does it relate to me? If you visualize each audience member as being stranded on a broken barge floating amid the ocean waves with no working rudder or steering mechanism, it becomes obvious that you must throw them a line to bring them back into shore. This "Why?" step is the connection that bridges the gap between you onstage, and your listeners in the audience. This is the next sixty seconds of your speech—the second most important part of your first impression—the next play you must definitely make in order to keep the momentum alive that was created in your introduction and carried on in the previous "Huh?" step.

The next "Why?" step is based on not only the bridge from your mind and heart to your audience members' minds and hearts, but it is also at the very core of leading, managing, coaching, teaching, parenting, inspiring, motivating, and persuading anyone for any occasion and for every reason. This is the first place you actually prove you are a professional speaker instead of just a professional presenter. "Why?" is when you first customize your message to the meeting theme, purpose, and audience. This is when you start making this time you are spending with your listeners relevant to their circumstances, jobs, industry, and lives. This most enlightening quote that is at the heart of sales, customer service, and especially public speaking is one I already quoted for a different reason in a previous chapter:

"The only place from which a person can grow is where he or she is. We must go where they are physically and emotionally." Only there can we gently persuade and instruct them to grow. Only there can we invite them to trust our character, listen, and learn from us.

Let us put both the "Huh?" attention getter and "Why?" connection bridging lines together for illustration: "One hundred thirteen teenagers were killed this weekend. Not one was drinking alcohol, but all died in drinking and driving accidents. Two teenagers from a town close by were driving home late when most bars are closing down, like Torre's just down the street, and a drunk guy ran a stop sign, hit them broadside going seventy miles an hour, and killed this 17-year-old kid and his high school sweetheart. Do any of you have teenagers? These two young friends were buried close to each other in the same cemetery."

Or, "A friend of mine, who is the proud father of nine children, killed his two youngest daughters last Wednesday. They were only eight and ten years old, and, as their father, he was responsible to make sure they were wearing their seat belts. On Wednesday my friend was a lousy dad. Because his little girls were not wearing their seat belts, when a car ran a stop sign and hit their car, his precious little angels were thrown out of the car and killed instantly. He got out of the hospital just in time to attend their funerals."

Because it is the speaker's responsibility to go out of their way to connect with each audience member and turn them into listeners, let me illustrate this "the only place we can connect with others is where they are" principle with a story.

MR. CROFT

I was recently visiting with Mr. Croft, my former high school teacher. We were discussing mutual respect and support in the context of positive discipline. I was looking for a firsthand experience from the world of education that would apply to parenting, coaching, and the corporate world of management, sales, and customer service.

The conversation centered on how to motivate, inspire, and empower others—not only to increase performance and productivity but to follow the rules and show respect. Mr. Croft asked for my definitions. With regard to mutual respect and support, I said, "The only place from which a person can grow is where he or she is." As for positive discipline, I said, "You cannot increase a person's performance by making him or her feel worse; humiliation immobilizes behavior." Mr. Croft's eyes lit up with excitement as he shared the following experience to illustrate this point. "I had a student who disrupted everything," he said.

"Did you send him to the office?" I asked.

With an offended look on his face, he said, "I've taught school for over twenty-five years and I've never sent a student to the principal." Mr. Croft laughed. "Most of my colleagues think the principal has all the Band-Aids. No way. Teachers are responsible for their classrooms and the development and education of each kid. You don't just throw them out when they do something wrong. We have to invite them to grow. We must catch them doing something right."

"Mr. Croft," I interrupted, "I've been to schools where a long line of students trails out the principal's office, down the hall, out the door and past the 9A bus stop. They're suntanned! And they just stand there with that look of 'yep, I screwed a goldfish into the pencil sharpener four months ago and I'm still waiting to see the principal.' If this is education, we're fooling ourselves! So what did you do with your student?" "Interesting you should ask," he replied. "I didn't give up on him.

My research uncovered that this James character played in a rock-and-roll band and that he was playing that Friday night in a smoke-filled, honky-tonk, redneck biker bar out in the bushes somewhere. I talked five teachers into going with me in case I needed backup."

"Then what happened?" I asked.

"Now picture this," Mr. Croft continued. "Six of us in argyle sweaters with matching socks stood at the back of the dance floor surrounded by teenagers who looked like they'd been mugged with a staple gun. The lead singer had a carburetor stuck in his nose. When James spotted us he leaned into the microphone and asked, 'What are you proctologist-looking teachers doing here?' We told him we heard his band was awesome and wanted to check them out. My colleagues and I only stayed fifteen minutes. That's all the noise we could take."

That was Friday night. On Monday morning was James a discipline problem in Mr. Croft's class? No way. Was he a problem in Mr. Croft's class for the rest of the school year? No way! Was James a discipline problem in other teachers' classrooms for the rest of the school year? Yes! Was it because they couldn't teach? No. It was simply because they didn't care!

Positive discipline means caring about a person physically and emotionally—and catching that person doing something right!

HOW?

Give me the proof! Tell me the stories. Share the emotional, funny, and thought-provoking experiences and researched data that give me the hope that I can actually go from where I am to where I want to be. Help me see through illustrations that what one person or organization has done really is possible; that if I think and behave and believe and conceive the same as a specific champion did, I, too, can become a champion.

Stories and parables are the parts of the speech that grab and keep the attendees listening. They constitute the entertaining, emotional portion that they remember and can't wait to share with family, co-workers, and friends who did not hear you speak. This fourth "How?" step is best delivered through a process of "make a statement, make a point, and then use 'for instance' to sharpen your point." Then do it again. Make another point and illustrate it.

One of the most popular and easiest resources to illustrate "How?" is history. Because most presenters focus on the overused examples from history—such as Abraham Lincoln's failing his way to success and Edison discovering 999 ways that a light bulb won't work—why not dig up some new, unique "for instances"? Especially when you are given topics like racism. Instead of doing the predictable or focusing on the victims and negative struggles for equality, why not take the surprising, positive high road and use fascinating examples from history? Elijah McCoy was a gifted engineer who happened to be the son of slaves. During his lifetime he was awarded forty-five patents. In 1872, he invented a device to make steam engines run more smoothly. Because of the accepted level of rampant racism at this time in our history, the market resisted McCoy's invention – no doubt feeling it couldn't work if it was designed by a black man. But competitors couldn't match his results, so buyers began asking, "Is this the real McCoy?"

INVENTIONS FROM BLACKS

Paper—Africans
Alphabet —Africans
Stainless-steel pads—Alfred Benjamin

Ironing board—Sarah Boone
Horseshoe—Oscar E. Brown
Lawn mower—John A. Burr
Typewriter—Burridge & Marshman
Peanut butter—George W. Carver
Soap and lotion—George W. Carver
Window cleaner—A. L. Lewis
Pencil sharpener—John L. Love
Fire extinguisher—Tom J. Marshal
Toilet —T. Elkins
Guitar—Robert Flemming Jr.
Air conditioner—Frederick M. Jones
Internal combustion engine—Frederick M. Jones
Refrigerator—J. Standard
Mop—T. W. Stewart
Folding chair—Purdy & Sadgwar
Baby buggy—W. H. Richardson
Lawn sprinkler—J. W. Smith

Women don't get enough credit for the part they played in the American Revolution. We've all heard of Betsy Ross and how she made the first American flag, but women have been in the thick of things since the beginning. One brave young woman was only sixteen when she took a midnight ride as dangerous and exciting – but far less publicized – as Paul Revere's.

On the night of April 25, 1777, two thousand British soldiers began destroying rebel storehouses. They found rum among the supplies, got drunk and started burning the town. A wounded messenger rode to a farm twenty miles from the town. The man who lived on the farm was the captain of the local militia. If he left to warn the surrounding cities, he would not be able to lead his 400 volunteers into battle.

His daughter, Sybil, offered to go in his place. Mounted sidesaddle, she rode forty miles – twice as far as Paul Revere – through a perilous region filled with hostile Indians. As she traveled, she shouted warnings and banged on doors with a stout branch to alert the townspeople along the way. It took Sybil all night to make her ride.

EMOTIONAL CONNECTION

The choreography of emotion can never be perceived as a cavalier way to manipulate another's thoughts and feeling. If this is the purpose of your story, poem, or comments, I guarantee your audience members will see right through it, feel violated, and turn you off for the rest of your speech.

However, if you take them to a certain high level through laughter, you are subconsciously given the right to take them to an equally low level in tears, as long as you don't keep them hurting. In other words, if your words make someone hurt, it's okay as long as you also help them heal. Let us never back down from the reality that the things we hate to hear the most are usually the things we need to hear the most.

Failure is an event, not a person. There is a huge difference between the person and the performance. You invite your listeners to feel and internally excavate their personal lives through your stage-conducted self-audit. To assure you that it's okay and actually very responsible of you as a speaker to go deeper and perhaps even open up some old wounds in your listeners' past and present lives, let me share this medical understanding on healing.

SPEAKER AS HEALER

When we understand medicine and music from the inside-out perspective, it is easy to fully comprehend the process of healing. We all know that doctors can't and don't heal anyone. Through the administration of medication and the performance of surgery, they help us heal ourselves. Physicians are not gods or miracle workers; they are catalysts and caregivers. Having said this, let's clarify the process of healing. There are two kinds of healing – healing by "First Intention" and by "Second Intention."

Healing by the First Intention

Outside healing is where there is a scratch or superficial, shallow wound with a straight edge opening that quickly coagulates, stops bleeding, and heals with a few stitches to close the cut or with just a Band-Aid to keep it clean. Name-calling, gossip, and rumors are "scuffed knees" and "paper cuts" that can and will always heal from the outside in.

Healing by Second Intention

Inside out healing is where the wound is deep, the edges jagged, and the gouge uncertain. In this case if you only stop the surface bleeding, stitch the surface layer of skin, and bandage it to heal from the outside in, underneath it all and unbeknownst to you, the wound is festering, infection is setting in, and gangrene could result in the amputation of that limb. When we suffer and experience a deep gouge wound – a stabbing, the bursting of our appendix, a broken heart, the loss of a loved one, a devastating divorce, being let go from a job – the only way we can heal is if we keep the wound open long enough with the proper treatment – kindness and care – until it can slowly, in its own time, heal from the inside out, one layer, one step at a time.

A professional speaker does this by sharing a heart-warming story that reopens a deep wound in an audience member. They keep the deep wound open just long enough to let some healing occur, but then, because they are in a public setting, the professional speaker closes the wound by providing comic relief immediately afterward.

This "How?" middle section of the speech that offers the "for instances" is the glue that binds the introduction, which states you're an expert in this or a master storyteller or are personally experienced, to the first 60 seconds of your attention-getting "Huh?" and to the follow-up minute that answers, "Why bring that up?"

Something as redundant as speaking on drinking and driving, which has been crammed down young people's throats for decades, can actually be presented in a powerful, emotionally stirring, less preachy, more sharing way when we take full advantage of this "How" step and utilize the long-lasting third party approach found in a story or a poem:

MAKE THE MUNDANE COME ALIVE

Steve was careful about his drinking because his wife, Melba, worried. She said liquor made him too confident and not cautious. *Women never really understand their men*, he thought. Instead, they always worry about things that never happen. Steve snapped up the shot glass, tilted his head, and nodded to the bartender as he left.

Outside he thought about how happy he was. Steve owned a house and Melba was pregnant again. He hoped it would be a girl since they already had an 18-month-old son. Steve was hurrying to pick up Melba at the doctor's office. Although the car skidded slightly on the icy roads, he wanted to hurry since he'd stopped at the bar. He sped up a notch, then suddenly realized he couldn't make the turn at the bottom of the hill. The car was headed for the guardrail that was set around the edge of the lake. To compensate, Steve propped his door open with his briefcase so he could get out when the car hit. He planned to jump out and swim to the bank.

People saw the car coming and watched as it splashed into the water. As he planned, Steve got out safely and swam for shore. People cheered when he arrived safely. He thought, *See, I can handle my liquor.* As he stood there smiling, waving to the crowd, and watching his car submerge, Steve's heart sank. His little boy, Jared, was still strapped in his car seat in the back of the car.

SHOCK FACTOR

Shock factor is an extremely effective way to illustrate a mundane topic like Stop, Look and Listen before you act:

Alaskan Trapper

An Alaskan trapper lost his wife and was left to care for his two-year-old daughter. At times he had to leave the little girl with his faithful dog so he could work in the woods. While away one afternoon a terrible blizzard came up. The trapper was forced to take refuge in a hollow tree. At daybreak he rushed to his cabin and found the door was open. His dog was covered with blood. There was no little girl anywhere. The father was terrified that something awful had happened. Fearful that his dog had killed and eaten his child, the trapper reached for his ax.

In one swift move he smashed the skull of his loyal and trusted canine companion. Like a maniac he tore through the cabin searching for his missing girl. Suddenly a faint cry came from under the bed. There was his daughter, safe and sound. Looking further he found the bloody remains of a wolf in the corner. Then he knew— the dog had saved the child from the fangs of the wolf. If he had only stopped to assess the situation rationally, the trapper could have held both his child and his dog in his arms.

Weigh all factors before you make a move. Those who act hastily regret their actions later. It happens all the time. Judgments made irrationally are clouded by a lack of information. The whole picture is hazy. So get the facts before you act. The flip side of these heart-wrenching stories is an equally instructive use of a song:

SPECIAL MAN

(Dan Clark Copyright 1985)

A little boy wants to be like his dad
So he watches us night and day.
He mimics our moves and weighs our words.
He steps in our steps all the way.

He's sculpting a life we're the model for.
He'll follow us happy or sad,
And his future depends on example set
'Cause the little boy wants to be just like his dad.

A special man talks by example,
Takes the time to play and hug his lad.
A special man walks by example,
The very best friend a growing boy ever had.
Any male can be a father -
But it takes a special man to be a dad.

He needs a hero to emulate.
He breathes 'I believe in you.'
Would we have him see everything we see
And have him do what we do?

When we see the reverence that sparkles and shines
In the worshipping eyes of our lad,

Will we be at peace if his dreams come true
And he grows up to be just like his dad?
Yes, a special man talks by example,
Takes the time to play and hug his lad.
A special man walks by example,
The very best friend a growing boy ever had.
Any male can be a father –
But it takes a special man to be a dad.

This "How" step moves us to change our thinking and kicks us in the butt, encouraging us to think before we act and look inside for happiness. Why is the grass always greener somewhere else? Some people spend their whole lives looking for happiness when it's right under their noses. Teenagers run away looking for a better life, but they rarely find it. Divorce is rampant. The truth is happiness is where you are—you make your own.

Look Before You Leave

In the mid-1800s, a man sold his ranch in northern California to look for gold nuggets. The new owner put a mill on a stream that ran through the property. One day, the new owner's little girl brought home some sand from the stream in a jar and sifted through it. In the sand were the first shiny nuggets of gold to be found in California. If the man had stayed put, he could have had all the gold he ever needed. Since that day, $38 million in gold has been taken out of those few acres he sold.

It's better to try to make the most of what you have before trying to find happiness elsewhere. Maybe what can really make you happy is just hidden from your sight, temporarily out of view for a while. So look hard. Dig in where you are before you sell. Study the problems that might be pushing you away from your loved ones before you leave something very important behind.

Use Illustrations Everybody Can Relate To

"How?" brings the magic into the moment. Therefore, amid all of these shocking stories, it is critical to remind you not only of the importance of humor and that we all love to laugh a heck of a lot more than we want to cry but also that a speech structured, crafted, and written so listeners like it and will never forget it must have a funny story for every sad one.

"He who laughs, lasts." It's a medical fact that if you keep your sense of humor, you'll probably live longer. Even large corporations realize the truth in it. Monsanto, the chemical giant, hired a humor consultant to work with research scientists. Productivity increased 50 percent. Digital Equipment designed a Grouch Patrol to make funny faces at grumpy workers. Productivity went up; absenteeism went down. Bertrand Russell said, "One of the symptoms of an approaching nervous breakdown is the belief that one's work is terribly important." So lighten up!

Two of my favorite humorous observations are:

1. I'm losing hair on top of my head and growing it in my nose and ears. My only hope is that the hair in my right ear will grow long enough so I can comb it up over my head and fake everybody out.

2. I don't understand bowling. You take a big heavy ball, cram two fingers and a thumb into holes you might not ever get them out of, take four Fred Flintstone twinkle-toes steps, roll the ball, sit down, eat a hot dog, slurp a drink, and for this you need special shoes? And because they think we're going to steal the shoes, they make us leave a cash deposit. I don't know about you, but I don't own a green and purple shirt that's going to match those goofy shoes, and I definitely don't want to be seen walking around town with an 11½ on the back of my foot!

WHERE?

"**Where**" is the performance/entertainment component of your speech that causes your audience members to sit on the edge of their seats because they don't want to miss any part of your show. They constantly wonder, "Where will he take me next?"

Taking an audience on an exciting, emotional, up-and-down roller coaster ride is an art and requires special skills. These are the "mechanical moves" and "tangible tools" that polish the performance. They constitute the differentiating factors between a professional presenter and a consummate Hall of Fame speaker. In the Kentucky Derby, all horses are thoroughbreds. However, amidst all the champions entered in the race, only one wins this run for the roses and is crowned Derby winner. So likewise, there are a lot of professional speakers, but to be one of the best of the best and right for every audience, industry, and occasion, you need to perfect everything mentioned and taught in this book.

"**Where**" is also about, "Where do I go from here? Where is this system of success that others have used, which, if I also use, will work for me?" The system is a quantified, numbered formula or process such as the famous Twelve-Step Program of Alcoholics Anonymous. In this "Where?" step, you simply use your credibility to convince your listeners that neither an individual nor an organization can change with just a one-hour keynote speech, that training is not an expense, but rather an investment in the present and future of the organization. "Where?" is the place in the speech when you give out your website and explain that if they are serious about taking themselves to the next level, they will join you at your weekend seminar or retreat, buy your book, and bring you back for a full day of leadership, team building, sales, or customer service training. Because you firmly believe in what you are passionately persuading your listeners to do, you shamelessly offer everyone your products and follow-up services. You absolutely know you can change people's minds and show them how to become everything they were born to be!

As you now realize, audience members are craving a sustainable, emotional, personal experience—not just a speech. They don't want a presenter to deliver a talking-head monologue. They want to be part of an inspirational conversation where they feel you are genuinely there to help them become better, and because of this connection they want to maintain contact with you in every way available. This is why we should unashamedly offer our recorded and written resources to them.

WHEN?

"**When**?" is the conclusion that ties a bow around your speech. The "**When**?" step is "When are you going to do something with what I've just talked about?" It's the call to action. We don't learn to know; we learn to do. It doesn't do us any good to know how to read if we never pick up a book and read it. It doesn't do us any good to listen to a speaker if we never accept their challenge to change. It doesn't do a speaker any good to speak for sixty minutes with a great opening and great illustrations if they leave their listeners hanging in the air. "That's it? He's done? The speech is over? So what? He's 'left the building' and I have no new direction or clearer path to walk when I leave this meeting."

"**When**?" is the challenge. It's not the proverbial "meaningful poem." It's a direct invitation for each listener to immediately do something with what they have felt and heard, learned and assimilated into their souls. In the "How?" step we encouraged the making of a point and the sharpening of that point with illustrations, historical stories, and statistics.

Now we come to the conclusion of the speech. The very end of your speech, like the end of the proverbial pencil, should have a point. The conclusion must be more than a review of your "for instances." It must be more than a graceful exit off stage. And most definitely it should never be a cutesy gimmick to get people to give you a standing ovation.

EMOTIONAL CLOSE

Usually the one idea and feeling that your audience members remember most is their last impression. Consequently, I usually close my speeches in a mellow, inspirational way that allows the listeners to re-enter the outside world reality with a smooth transition. As an audience member myself, I personally enjoy an emotional, heartfelt, deeply moving story that illustrates once and for all the bottom line message of the speech, or a powerful quote that stirs a call to action. Consider the emotional impact of the following story I affectionately refer to as "Bopsy":

"BOPSY"

Bopsy was a young boy living in Phoenix, Arizona, dying of terminal leukemia. At the present time there is absolutely no cure. One day his mother had the presence of mind to ask him, "Bopsy, if you had one wish, what would it be?" Without even thinking about it, Bopsy replied, "Mommy, if I had one wish and I knew it would come true, I'd want to be a fireman."

The next morning, Bopsy's mother phoned the local fire department and talked to the fire chief. She explained her son's health condition and his wish. The fire chief had a heart as big as a house and answered, "I'd love to make Bopsy's dream come true. You tell him that we'll be by to pick him up at 8 a.m. We'll make him honorary fire chief for the whole day." The fire chief continued, "If you'll give me Bopsy's measurements, I'll have a helmet made for him just like the big guys wear. We'll have a yellow slicker jacket and rubber galoshes for him too."

Sure enough, at 8 a.m the fire engine pulled up in front of Bopsy's house. They helped him get all decked out in his very own fireman's uniform, and that day he got to go on two fire calls. It inspired him to the depth of his being, so that he lived three months longer than any doctor thought he could possibly live.

On the last night of Bopsy's short life, the head nurse in the hospital was monitoring his vital signs and noticed they were starting to weaken. Bopsy's parent's eyes filled with tears, as they knew his short life was coming to an end. Scrambling to help in any way she could, the nurse remembered the relationship Bopsy had developed with the local fire department. Immediately she phoned the fire chief and told him, "Bopsy is not doing too good and I thought you would like to know. Maybe there is something you could do for him."

The fire chief shouted, "You tell that little guy to hang on. We will be there in five minutes. But, nurse, there are a couple of things we need you to do for us. Will you please announce over the PA system of the hospital that everyone is going to hear the sirens screaming and see the lights flashing, and that we are coming to see our boy Bopsy for the last time. And would you please open up the third-story window to Bopsy's hospital room, because this time we're coming by hook and ladder!"

Moments later the sirens were screaming, the lights were flashing, and the fire engines pulled up to the hospital. A huge ladder went up the side of the building. Ten firemen and two firewomen scampered up the ladder and climbed through the third-story window into Bopsy's hospital room. They kissed him and cuddled him. With tears streaming down everyone's cheeks, the big, burly fire chief leaned over Bopsy's hospital bed and took hold of his frail little hand. With a big smile on his precious, innocent face, Bopsy looked up at the fire chief and with his last breath asked, "Chief, am I now really a fireman?"

The fire chief answered, "Bopsy, you are." And the little guy died. An awesome emotional close, eh? But only if you link it back into the chain of points and stories you've shared. For example, my conclusive commentary would be: "Can you now see and feel the power of a dream? I know this story of Bopsy resonates with everyone, young and old, because each of us has a dream stuck inside still unfulfilled. So, I guess the concluding question is, "What are you going to do about your dream?" It's like they say in the movie *South Pacific*, "If you don't have a dream, how ya gonna make a dream come true?"

CALL TO ACTION

Always conclude by asking your listeners for some specific action that is within their current capacity and personal power to perform: Dream! Believe! Vote! Forgive! Join! Participate! Execute! Buy! Improve! Love! Serve! Lead! Follow! Become more of who you already are—not because it is expected by others, but because it is demanded of yourself.

CHAPTER FOURTEEN

WHAT ARE THE EIGHT SCIENTIFIC ELEMENTS OF ORGANIZING AN EXTRAORDINARY PRESENTATION?

SPEECH ELEMENT 1 "OUTSIDE INTRODUCTION"

The Outside Introduction is your official introduction to your audience, written by you, and presented to your audience by someone credible in the organization with the sole purpose of getting everyone to listen to you. Because you are expected to begin and conclude your speech/sales presentation/remarks at a specific designated time, it is critical that you see your Outside Introduction as part of your speech, which means you don't want the person introducing you to deviate from what you have written. Therefore, it needs to be short, concise, fascinating, attention-getting, engaging, compelling, flattering, comprehensive, yet to the point, with the emphatic request that whoever reads it to the audience, has practiced it and agrees to read it word for word. In other words, take this Speech Element and assignment very seriously!

Begin by using this template to create a three-page document, writing a revealing paragraph on your knowledge, understanding and personal experience in each of the eight aspects of life. Start by taping into your memory bank and 'regurgitating' significant emotional events from your past and from your current and present reality. And because you shouldn't spend time writing a speech until you have spent enough time preparing yourself to speak, you also need to have an exciting, stretching and exhilarating active 'bucket list' that allows you to keep your speech fresh and exciting because you are! Conclude each paragraph by sharing one 'life lesson' that you learned in each category:

Physical:

_____

Mental:

_____

Spiritual:

_____

Emotional:

_____

Social:

_____

Financial:

_____

Familial:

_____

Charitable:

_____

Edit this three-page self-audit essay into a one-page document where "every word pays its own way," controlling exactly what you want the audience to know about you that builds your credibility in answering the first of three questions in Dan's "Speaker's Triangle": Why Should I Listen To You?

Type out this introduction in Times Roman, 14-point, bold font in paragraph format with paragraph spaces and Justified borders as an easy-to-read document.

At the top of this one sheet print the following two lines:

OFFICIAL INTRODUCTION FOR_____

(Please Read As Written)

OFFICIAL DAN CLARK INTRODUCTION)

Our speaker is Dan Clark – Husband, Father, Entrepreneur, CEO, Author, University Professor, Athlete, Adventurer, Songwriter, Recording Artist, Podcaster, Philanthropist, Patriot.

Dan studied Psychology at the University of Utah, founded a multi-million-dollar international communications firm, is a New York Times best-selling author of 37 books, a primary contributing author to the Chicken Soup for the Soul series, and an award-winning athlete who fought his way back from a paralyzing injury that cut short his football career.

Dan has been inducted into the Professional Speakers Hall of Fame, named one of the Top Ten Motivational Speakers in the World, has been featured in Forbes, Entrepreneur, Inc, Success, Sports Illustrated and Mayo Clinic Magazines, and has appeared on over 500 TV and radio programs including Oprah, Glenn Beck, and NPR.

Dan has delivered more than 5500 speeches, to millions of people, in all 50 states, in 76 countries, to most of the Fortune 500, Super Bowl Champions, United Nations and to our combat troops in Iraq, Afghanistan, Asia and Africa.

Dan's extraordinary life includes soaring to the edge of space in a U2 Reconnaissance aircraft, flying fighter jets with the Air Force Thunderbirds, racing automobiles at Nürburgring, and serving as a Pentagon appointee on the National Civic Leaders Board with the Secretary of the Air Force, and on the Board of Visitors of the Air Force Academy.

Dan has received America's three highest Civilian Awards presented by the President of the United States and the Secretary of Defense! But most important to Dan, he was named Utah Father of the Year!

Please welcome a funny man with a serious message – Dan Clark

ORGANIZATIONAL BREAKDOWN OF DAN'S OFFICIAL INTRO

After you write it – and edit so every word pays its own way - Print this Introduction on your Letterhead in Times New Roman, 14-point, bold font in paragraph format with line spaces at 1.15 and Justified Borders as an easy-to-read document.

OFFICIAL INTRODUCTION FOR (your name)
(Please Read As Written)

1st Paragraph: **Snapshot Bullet Point Bio** *(An Expert Worth Listening To)*
     Our speaker is Dan Clark – Husband, Father, Entrepreneur, CEO, Author, University Professor, Athlete, Adventurer, Songwriter, Recording Artist, Podcaster, Philanthropist.

2nd Paragraph: **Education/Credibility Boosters** *(An Expert Who Has Done What He Teaches)*

Dan studied Psychology at the University of Utah, founded a multi-million-dollar international communications firm, is a New York Times best-selling author of 37 books, a primary contributing author to the Chicken Soup for the Soul series, and an award-winning athlete who fought his way back from a paralyzing injury that cut short his football career.

3rd Paragraph: **Awards/Media** *(An Expert I Need to Listen To)*

Dan was named An Outstanding Young Man of America, has been inducted into the Professional Speakers Hall of Fame, named one of the Top Ten Motivational Speakers in the World, has been featured in Forbes, Entrepreneur, Inc, Success, Sports Illustrated and Mayo Clinic Magazines, and has appeared on over 500 TV and radio programs including Oprah, Glenn Beck, and NPR.

4th Paragraph: **Experience** *(An Expert Others Listen To!)*

Dan has delivered more than 5500 speeches, to millions of people, in all 50 states, in 75 countries, to most of the Fortune 500, Super Bowl Champions, United Nations and to our combat troops in Iraq, Afghanistan, Asia and Africa.

5th Paragraph: **Living Your Message** *(A Fascinating Person Who Inspires Me To Dream!)*

Dan's extraordinary life includes soaring to the edge of space in a U2 Reconnaissance aircraft, flying fighter jets with the Air Force Thunderbirds, racing automobiles at Nürburgring, and serving as a Pentagon appointee on the National Civic Leaders Board with the Secretary of the Air Force.

6th Paragraph: **Special Recognition** *(A Wonderful Human Being I Want to Follow!)*

Dan has received America's three highest Civilian Awards presented by the President of the United States and the Secretary of Defense! But most important to Dan, he was named Utah Father of the Year!

7th Paragraph: **Signature Welcome** *(An Expert I Can't Wait To See And Hear!)*

Please welcome a funny man with a serious message – Dan Clark!

SPEECH ELEMENT 2 "INSIDE INTRODUCTION"

The first 30-120 seconds of your presentation are vital – because you never get a second chance to make a first impression. 70% of communication is non-verbal. Therefore, your energy, grooming, branding/clothing, confident walk, and big smile introduce you before you speak. Then, your opening lines must be congruent with what the listeners see.

COMMON PITFALLS

Never start a speech with:

'My name is this. I am from this university with these credentials. And today I am going to talk about this'

These first two things will be covered by the Outside Introduction. And if the speaker (you) reiterate them, you are making it about you. Remember, they are not there to hear you speak. They want 'Take Away' practical application steps to implement when they leave. Which means your opening lines need to immediately assure them you are there to 'bless, not impress!'

Therefore, if you are there to talk about diet, you would begin by making it about the audience saying, 'What if you made one small change to your diet that would add seven years to your life?' When you begin, 'I am here to talk about...' it's about you. But when you begin, 'You will learn... it's about you, you, you, and the transference of trust is underway!

THE FOUR PRIMARY WAYS TO BEGIN A SPEECH

Ask a Question.

You cannot, not answer a question. Example: Do you agree that some things are true whether you believe them or not? Do you agree that everybody is entitled to their own opinion, but nobody is entitled to the wrong facts? Do you agree that we shouldn't believe everything that we think? The moment you realize your thoughts are not facts... everything changes!

State a Startling Factoid.

Example: According to Dr. Herb True at the University of Notre Dame, 44% of sales professionals quit after the first sales call; 24% quit after the second call; 14% quit after the third call; and 12% quit after the fourth call. That's 94% of sales professionals who quit by the fourth sales call. Yet 85% of all sales are closed between the 5th and 12th sales calls.

Funny Factoid:

In the last 17 years, 114 people died in America while exercising in a gym. In that same 17-year period, only 1 person died while eating a donut. Choose your path to happiness wisely!

Tell a Joke.

Not just any joke, because if no one laughs, you bomb! Tell a joke with a message that is relevant to your topic, so if no one laughs, you don't bomb because it's simply one of your many illustrations that illuminate your message.

Example: 'When they were looking for a keynote speaker, they called the best-looking guy they knew. And he turned them down.

So, they called the most intelligent, most educated guy they knew. And he turned them down too. So, they called the most humble, gracious, loveable guy they knew. And hey! I couldn't turn them down three times in a row! So, I'm honored to be here!'

Joke with an Analogy

"When my Aunt Lucy was 63 years old, she started walking five miles every day. Now she's 91 and we don't know where she is! Ha! We laugh, but the number one limiting belief that holds us back from accomplishing our goals is focusing on a future outcome, which creates worry, stress and anxiety - or dwelling in the past, which is like you are trying to rob your old house and you don't live there anymore! At the end of the day, the only question we can actually answer is: where are you right now? It's like ordering an Uber ride that requires you enter in your current location. And if you lie about where you are, the directions won't work!"

Start with a Story.

For example, I often share one of my most iconic stories that I wrote when I was thirteen years old, titled, **'Puppies for Sale'**:

A store owner was tacking a sign above his door that read 'Puppies for Sale.' Soon a little boy appeared and asked how much he was going to sell the puppies for?

The owner said, 'Anywhere from thirty to fifty dollars.' To that the boy reached into his pocket, pulled out some change and replied, 'I have two dollars and thirty cents. Can I please look at them?

The owner smiled and whistled, and out of the kennel came Lady, running down the aisle of his store, followed by five tiny puppies – one lagging considerably behind. Immediately, the boy singled out the limping puppy and asked, 'What's wrong with that dog?' The owner explained that it didn't have a hip socket and it would always be lame.

Excitedly the boy replied, 'That's the puppy that I want to buy.' The owner said, 'No, you don't want to buy that little dog. If you really want him, I'll just give him to you.'

The little boy got upset, looked straight into the storeowner's eyes, pointed his finger, and said, 'I don't want you to just give him to me. That little dog is worth every bit as much as all the other dogs and I'll pay full price. In fact, I'll give you two dollars and thirty cents now and fifty cents a month until I have him paid for.'

The owner countered, 'You really don't want to buy this little dog. He is never going to be able to run and jump and play with you like the other puppies.'

To this, the little boy reached down and rolled up his pant leg to reveal a badly twisted, crippled left leg supported by a big metal brace. He looked up at the storeowner and softly replied, 'Well, I don't run so well myself, and this little puppy will need someone who understands.'

FIRST 30 SECONDS / FIRST THREE TO FIVE MINUTES

The next three to five minutes of your presentation is also considered part of this Inside Introduction because it sets the tone and establishes the expectation for the rest of your entire speech.

For example, if your assigned topic is wearing seat belts, you don't begin by saying, "I've been asked to talk about the importance of wearing your seat belt." Instead, you could start your speech by saying, "A friend of mine, who is the proud father of nine children, killed his two youngest daughters last Wednesday.

As their father, he was responsible for making sure they were wearing their seat belts. When he ran a stop sign as a distracted driver and got hit and T-boned by a truck, his precious little girls (eight and ten years old) were not wearing their seat belts and were thrown out of the car and killed instantly. He got out of the hospital just in time to attend their joint funeral. I will never forget the conflict of emotions in that tear-jerking memorial service, feeling devastated and sad that the little girls were dead, while feeling angry that my friend, who was usually a great father, was a lo and purpose for speaking.

A thesis statement is the first thing you create when writing a speech. When you create your thesis statement first, it will help you narrow down your topic and focus on the ideas you want to get across to your audience. A two-sentence statement summarizes the entire message and your conclusive premise.

For example, if your speech topic is money management, you know your main ideas are pay off debt, save, invest, improve quality of life, prepare for emergencies, and have a retirement account. To create a thesis statement, start with your specific purpose statement: "I want to persuade my audience to use money management techniques.'

Next, remove the first part of your purpose statement so it now simply says: 'To use money management techniques.' When you know your speech is on a college campus, your finely tuned purpose statement becomes: 'College students should manage their money.'

Next, incorporate your main ideas into your thesis statement, which now becomes: 'College students should manage their money now so they can pay off debt, save, invest, improve quality of life, prepare for emergencies, and have a retirement account.'

Because the Thesis Statement accurately identifies the focus of the topic and summarizes your message, it serves as the 'bookend' statement that ties a bow around your entire speech by ending your presentation the same way as you began. When you do, your listeners not only remember the main points of your speech, but they can and will share it with others at work, home, and play!

SPEECH ELEMENT 4 "STRUCTURE"

Because there will be people in every audience who subscribe to one of the two learning styles – left brain, cognitive, cerebral, fact-based, non-emotional; or the right brain, relational, touchy-feely, interpretation of the facts-based, emotional style, it is critical that you organize your speech/presentation into a 'Structured Template' using either an Acronym, Sequential Numbering System, Creative Road Sign Markers, or a catchy metaphor. Structuring your speech/presentation accomplishes three things:

Creating an Acronym, Numbering System, list of Road Sign Markers, or metaphor helps you decide on the sequential order in which you present your material, which allows you to 'choreograph' the ebb and flow of your presentation. This Structure allows every audience member to keep track of where you are in your presentation, which captivates their interest to the end.

The time-tested marketing 'Rule of Three' proves that we remember information best when it is presented in sets of Three. The most memorable brands use three words in their Tag Line:

The Three Elements of Storytelling

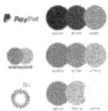

Use three Colors to create your Brand Color Palette. Use three 'Acts' to create stories for your brand, whether you're seeing logos or hearing Tag Lines, information in Three's stick! Use Three Acronym Letters, or three numbers/road signs, or a metaphor to create your speech Structure, such as my three-letter Acronym I created from my book title: The Art of Significance, turning the word Art into the acronym A.R.T. - representing Awareness, Refinement, and Transformation. Or a Three-Legged Stool, Equilateral Triangle, the three Olympic Medals: Gold, Silver, Bronze, the Olympic Motto: Citius, Altius, Fortius, or the three university degrees: Bachelor's, Master's, Doctorate.

Hilarious Suggestion:

If your chosen 'Structure' is an acronym, you could introduce your system with humor by saying, "To guide you through my process, I have created an acronym. And trust me, I am sensitive to acronyms, so it's not a long one. Last week, I heard the President of Yale University speak and use the university as his acronym, stating, 'Y stands for,' and he went on for 30 minutes. 'A stands for,' and he went on for another 30 minutes. Just then, the guy sitting next to me whispered, 'Thank God he didn't go to the Massachusetts Institute of Technology, or we would be here all day!" Ha!

SPEECH ELEMENT 5 "SOCIAL PROOF"

Jokes with a message, humorous stories, interviews with gurus and celebrities that allow you to teach what works, what doesn't, and why, and especially your own inspirational experiences. You should spend less time preparing a speech and more time preparing yourself to speak, continuously adding to your 'bucket list' to meet interesting influential people, visit extraordinary places, and accomplish amazing things.

Part of Social Proof is remembering that the listener doesn't relate to our perfections (if we even have any). The listener relates to our imperfections. They don't really care if we have succeeded. They want to know if we have ever fallen and failed, and what we did about it to learn from our mistakes and get back up and go again. In the context of all Eight Elements to an Organized Presentation, by far Social Proof is the single most significant element because it provides the inspiration and motivation that answers the second question in Dan's Speaker's Triangle – Can I Do It Too?

Each of the letters in your Structured Acronym, Number System, or system of Road Sign Markers requires one powerful inspirational story/cutting-edge example and unforgettable illustration to drive home the point you are making as a true-to-life reason why your listener can also do it too.

Powerful Suggestion

Because we should spend less time preparing a speech and more time preparing ourselves to speak, you must keep three ongoing, always-growing lists in a written journal.

- The first list is an ongoing collection of funny things people have said, great jokes you've heard, and humorous stories that make a point. Practice telling each of these jokes and hilarious anecdotes ten times to make sure they are logged away in your brain to be used whenever the occasion arises.

- The second list is a collection of quotes you've heard or researched that make you think and feel. Commit to memorizing one quote every day so they become more than just entertainment – they become part of your vocabulary.

- The third list is a collection of your personal stories and significant emotional events that have created your beliefs. Evaluate the life lessons learned. Edit so 'every word pays its own way.' Then replace the verbs with action verbs that are more colorful and descriptive. Add humor and emotion to each story. Now practice telling each story ten times so it is locked in your mind, so it is literally 'on call' whenever the situation calls for it.

SPEECH ELEMENT 6 "RESEARCHED DATA BASED STATISTICS"

This element not only draws in and keeps the left brain, cognitive learners engaged in your speech/presentation, but it builds your overall credibility as an expert in this particular topic, proving to your listeners that what you are sharing is much more than just your opinion. You always include one researched data-based statistic or edited case study to validate each point you have in your 'Structured' Acronym, Numbering System, Road Signs, or Metaphor.

SPEECH ELEMENT 7 "VISUAL AID SUPPORT"

PowerPoint slide presentations are misused and abused in two ways: First, they are used as a crutch by presenters who are insecure speaking in public or unprepared and must narrate the slides to stay on track. For this reason, Visual Aids usually do more harm than good because they create a barrier between you and your audience. Every time a listener looks at a screen, you lose your intimate connection with them and invite them to stop listening.

Second, the creator of the slides crams too much information onto one slide so no one can read it past the third row!

If you decide to use PowerPoint or a video clip, make sure the slides are a minimum of words in a large type font, and the video is edited down to minimum length, with a 'black slide' inserted into the presentation immediately after each slide or video, which forces the audience members to stop looking at the screen and again focus on you in an eye to eye, heart-to-heart, connected conversation.

SPEECH ELEMENT 8 "CONCLUSION / CALL TO ACTION"

The Conclusion is different than the Call to Action. Do Not Conclude by just fizzling out and walking off. And no matter what, do Not end your speech with a Question-and-Answer session, which allows someone who disagrees with you to hijack your message and take you down a controversial 'rabbit hole.' If you offer a Q&A in a 60-minute keynote, bring it to a close with ten minutes left in your speech, so you can bring everybody back on course and conclude in your prepared, practiced, powerful way!

The Conclusion needs to circle back to Element #3 'Thesis,' which reminds your audience about the Promised Benefits of listening to you for the last hour and validates that you kept your promise!

Every 'Conclusion' must always be emotional – using an evocative poem or arousing music that generates claps and cheers; or sharing a deeply inspiring story that brings your listener to their knees; or a clever quip that gets their attention and is easily remembered: "Drink, Swear, Steal, and Lie. Drink from the fountain of truth, knowledge, and wisdom that is constantly flowing around you. Steal a little time each day to do something special for someone when you know you won't get the credit. Swear to make this the best day of your life so far – it may be your last. And when you lie down tonight, thank God above that you are free and have the ability to dream mighty dreams and make them come true!

Too many presenters focus on the presentation instead of on the desired outcome. Anybody can make a speech – the goal is to close the deal, focus and finish, and inspire them to do something with the experience they just heard, saw, and felt.

In the Call to Action, remember that we need to create trust and connect with our listeners as someone who is not a 'sales agent,' but a 'Sales Assistant/Sales Advisor.' Three time-tested phrases include:

1. "Here is what I know, and here is what I am still trying to figure out." This comes off as being super genuine and shows that by admitting there are things you don't know, they take what you do know more seriously and take action.

2. "I want to make sure you have all the facts before you make your decision." This shows you care about them more than what the outcome might be and builds instant credibility.

3. "Take your time. There is no pressure from me." This shows patience and that you don't want them to make a rash decision, which makes you someone who has their best interest at heart.

CHAPTER FIFTEEN

WHAT IS THE SCIENCE BEHIND A PERSUASIVE SPEECH?

"Reason leads to conclusions, but it is emotion that leads to action."

A persuasive speech is designed to influence, convince, motivate, sell, inspire, and stimulate the audience members to take action about a topic both interesting and relevant to their life.

When you try to change others' attitudes or behavior, you need to base your persuasive effort on some guiding principles. This requires an understanding of how and why people change their minds.

A strong grasp of purpose is especially important in persuasive speaking. When you try to change people, and not simply educate or inspire them, you are more likely to encounter resistance.

Your purpose must be clearly distinguished between seeking to actually change behavior and trying to influence beliefs and attitudes. If the audience is a favorable group, who views you as "one of them" (an athlete, a sales professional, someone from their same industry or religious persuasion) they will not raise counter arguments for you to deflect or defuse, which means you focus on strengthening their attitudes and take them from belief into positive action.

PERSUASION VS. INSTRUCTION / SPEECH VS. LECTURE

At the end of the day, there are really only two types of speeches: Persuasive Sales and Instructive Education. Though both forms of presentation (written and spoken) consist in telling—and telling is salways teaching—the difference between the emotion of sales talk, the non-emotional lecture, and other forms of instructive speech is that one aims at affecting the action or feelings of the listeners, while the other aims at affecting their minds. Both involve persuasion, but for a different purpose.

In the original meaning of the term "lecture," the lecturer was first of all a reader. Today, lecturing is still an oral or spoken presentation closely associated with writing out a speech and then reading it aloud. Some think they are speakers when they use PowerPoint slides, but in reality they are presenters (which we will define in an upcoming chapter) following a previously written-out script. The major challenge in being a lecturer, or what I will hereafter refer to as a presenter, is that the ability to write effectively does not always go hand in hand with the ability to speak effectively. In fact, the contrary occurs more often than not.

Bottom line? Lecturers are presenters of information that instructs. It's the educator teaching math, the accountant explaining your taxes, the boring college professor whipping off Plan A with no voice inflection, or a military officer giving a briefing at a staff meeting for the sole purpose of imparting knowledge. Having said this, I believe that it is a direct violation of our responsibility and a blatant adulteration of the privilege of the platform if we are given an opportunity to speak and all we do is lecture in an instructive presentation. Print out your written essay and email it out. Don't waste our time reading or presenting something we can read for ourselves. Public speaking—in any location, for any reason, to any group—is to instruct and inform, but unless we are moved emotionally to take some kind of action after our time together is over, then our time together was a waste of time! Every presenter can become a speaker if they embrace Ethos, Pathos, Logos, persuasion, and instruction!

For this reason, and as we have reiterated before, whenever we are invited to speak, listeners should leave you not impressed with you and your achievements, but impressed with themselves and how much they have learned. They should leave you with a belief that if put in the same situation, they too could have done what you did and accomplish what you have done.

EMOTIONAL APPEALS FOR A FAVORABLE GROUP

The use of emotional appeals intensifies support for your purpose. The difference between commitment and action is emotional arousal. Out of the vast number of positions you agree with, there is a much shorter list of issues that you really care about. These issues appeal to your most basic needs, touch on your core values and have a personal, emotional effect on your life. Basic values include: patriotism, humanitarian charity, and making progress. Basic needs include: survival (housing, food, education, employment), security, and status (respect). Basic emotions include: fear, pity, and love.

In this context, the persuasive technique is to be very specific about how their lives are affected, and then to show them that their actions can and will make a difference (your check for $240 can pay for one cleft lip/cleft palate surgery that will change the life of one child forever)!

Invite audience members to make a public commitment, such as signing a petition or lending their name to a letterhead. People who are seen and heard by others – oral or written – are less likely to change their minds.

In a persuasive speech you don't "invite" people to participate – you specifically tell them what you want them to do. You don't say, "Stop by headquarters some time." You say, "Before you leave, I need you to sign up for your specific time to walk the precinct and make your ten phone calls."

In a persuasive speech it is important to prepare your audience to carry your message to others. Always inspire and influence and challenge and show how and why each audience member can become persuaders in their own right. This is accomplished by giving them the "ready tools and answers" necessary for them to authoritatively talk about your speech to neighbors, coworkers, family members, and friends who are neutral or hostile about politics, religion, prolife/pro-choice, sexual orientation, gun control, welfare, government bailouts, English as America's official language, illegal immigration, minimum wage, higher taxes/tax breaks, socialized medicine, or a flat tax like 10% tithing, where everyone gives the government the same portion of their income, etc., etc.

EMOTIONAL APPEALS FOR AN UNFAVORABLE GROUP

Establish common ground by using sound logic and presenting extensive evidence. Before you can expect people to agree with you they must have some comprehension of the issue. The main concern is clarity. It is critical that you clearly define the specifics with visual presentation aids if necessary, using examples, statistics, and revealing that you understand their side of the issue, quoting their statistics and their examples, with your side presented as the dominant and obvious, rational, and empathetic solution.

To maximize your persuasion, make a point (a one-sentence "thesis" statement) followed by a credible statistic, followed by an illustrative emotional story, then repeat this process with every point–thesis, statistic, story, until you have built an ironclad case supported by impeccable, unbiased evidence. With an unfavorable audience, you must clearly indicate every step of your reasoning.

Generally, it is a good idea to address counterarguments in addition to presenting your own viewpoints. On widely debated topics, these ideas will already be on listeners' minds, and they expect a response. At the end of your straightforward "pro" speech, your audience may agree with you. But if listeners later become aware of powerful opposing arguments, they may discredit your position.

INOCULATE YOUR LISTENERS AGAINST OPPOSING VIEWS

In a Persuasive Speech, believing that another speaker may disagree with our position, we should "inoculate" our audience by presenting a few counterarguments and answering them. Then, when these points are brought up later, the listeners will say, "Oh, yes, I was warned about this." Inoculation has created "antibodies" to resist the opposing position. In most cases, answer the counterarguments AFTER developing your own position. The only exception is when you know your listeners are so preoccupied with an opposing position that they can't concentrate on your message or there has been a crisis right before your speech, or a speaker who opposes your thesis has presented immediately before you, then you should answer the counter arguments toward the beginning of your speech.

STRONGEST POINTS FIRST OR LAST

Ideally, all of the arguments and support for your persuasive speech, purpose, and thesis statement should be strong. In reality, however, you will find that you must use materials of varying strength. These should not be arranged randomly. People will remember best what you say first and what you say last. In light of this, arranging your arguments either from weakest to strongest (climax) or from strongest to weakest (anti-climax) will be more effective than placing your best points in the middle.

Remember in every speech (especially in a Persuasive Speech), we must structure our remarks as a perfect airplane flight. We must have a perfect, fast, exhilarating, powerful takeoff, climb to our cruising altitude as quickly as possible, fly our audience (passengers) through the fog, storms and turbulence until we have smooth sailing. When the flight (speech) is over, give them a smooth landing at your agreed upon destination with a challenge to leave the airport (meeting) and go where they need to go and do what they need to do now that they have arrived and you have delivered them safely.

THE USE OF REASONING

Inductive Logic: The emphasis is on collecting observable data with a pattern of reasoning when your argument consists of combining your series of observations to lead to a probable conclusion. In other words, we believe that what has happened before will happen again. (We stop in front of oncoming traffic at an intersection because we believe from previous experience that the drivers will obey the traffic signals).

Deductive Logic: Consists of manipulating verbal statements or promises and rearranging things you already know to discover something meaningful about how they fit together, as in scientific breakthroughs, gossip, and the famous "English Scotland Yard Murder Mystery." In our everyday lives, we have that "aha!" experience when we suddenly discover the pattern underlying separate facts and realize their implication. In Deductive Reasoning, if your listeners accept the Thesis (promise) they must accept the conclusion. It is an all-or-nothing agreement. Therefore, in order for the conclusion to be absolute, the premise must be absolute.

Reasoning by Analogy: People intuitively look to similar examples when they want to understand something. However, do not con fuse a literal analogy with a figurative analogy. Frank Zappa, a legendary rock and roll star, was on a conservative TV talk show and the famously indignant host, who incidentally had an artificial leg, laid into Zappa's appearance. He said, "I guess your long hair makes you a woman." Zappa responded, "I guess your wooden leg makes you a table." The host lightened up!

CHAPTER SIXTEEN

WHAT IS THE SCIENCE BEHIND THE MOTIVATED SEQUENCE?

Developed by Alan Monroe, the Motivated Sequence is one of the most widely used organizers for persuasive speeches. Although your speech begins with the Outside and Inside Introductions, followed by your Thesis statement, the deepest connection between you and your listeners occurs when they progress through the five mental stages as they hear your speech:

Attention:
The speaker must first motivate the audience to listen to the speech.

Need:
Listeners must become aware of a compelling, personalized problem.

Satisfaction:
The course of action advocated must be shown to alleviate the problem.

Visualization:
Psychologically, it is important that the audience has a vivid picture of the benefits of agreeing with the speaker or the evils of the alternatives.

Action:
The speech should end with an overt call for the listeners to act.

AN EXAMPLE OF THE MOTIVATED SEQUENCE

Thesis: We need a light rail system in our county to reduce excessive commuter traffic congestion.

Attention: I left in plenty of time to get to work for my important meeting where I was making a presentation that would generate $18,000 for the company. I heard screeching brakes, a nd a crash. No one was hurt. But we sat there and waited, and waited and waited as the cars blocked two lanes of traffic. My mood went from irritation to outrage to despair. I arrived at work an hour late just as the meeting concluded!

Need: Excessive reliance on automobile transportation to the county's major employed areas is causing service problems:

    A. Major traffic jams
    B. Pollution
    C. Stress and missed meetings for commuters

Satisfaction: A light rail system should be constructed to alleviate these problems:

    A. Definition of a light rail
    B. Proposed route
    C. Proposed funding

Visualization: The new system would be a vast improvement:

    A. Free parking at the boarding point
    B. Time to relax, have a cup of coffee and read while traveling and leaving the driving to someone else
    C. Arrive home ready to be with family and friends
    D. Scenario without the light rail – increased traffic, gridlock, daily stress, work loss, pollution

Action: Support the county initiative for a light rail system. Vote for it. Ask your employer to commit to providing free shuttle service from the proposed light rail station to your place of business.

* Of the five steps in this Motivated Sequence to persuasion, the most important are Visualization and the Action step must be concrete.

** Using this six-step Motivated Sequence to organize your thoughts and research material, insert your information into the speech writing formula called, "Six Steps To Crafting A Speech Listeners Love": Shhh, Huh, Why, How, Where, When.

Thesis	Shhh
Attention	Huh
Need	Why
Satisfaction & Visualization	How
Action	Where & When

Using All Resources

Every persuasive speech should have at least three credible documented sources that you cite in your speech.

With all of these resources now at your fingertips, combine the "Six Steps to Crafting a Speech Listener's Love" and the "Eight Elements of an Organized Speech," to write your final edited and most spectacular speech!

CHAPTER SEVENTEEN

WHAT ARE THE FIFTEEN PLATFORM PERFORMANCE SKILLS AND ACCOMPANYING "STAGE TIPS"?

(To Do More Than Speak and Put On a Show)

1. Create an unofficial "meet and greet."

Because you show up an hour before the meeting starts for your "sound check" (where you meet the head of audio/visual and the person calling the show, check out where you enter and exit the stage, check the style of microphone and sound system, laptop, projector, lighting, and especially the person who is going to introduce you to make sure he/she has your typed out official introduction and agrees to read it verbatim), when meeting attendees start to arrive, position yourself so you can introduce yourself, shake their hands, look them in the eye and thank them for coming.

Make sure you go out of your way to talk to the people in the very back of the room because they are usually the ones who don't want to be there. If you create a relationship with them before you speak you have captured their attention at the beginning of your remarks, which means if they are on board, the rest of the crowd is usually on board. By engaging in this often overlooked activity of a meet and greet, you increase the odds of everybody cheering you on from the beginning of your speech – which is the most critical "Inside Introduction."

2. Smile and immediately get eye contact with your audience members.

Listeners like to feel they are influencing what you say. Audience reaction is an essential ingredient in this whole business of speaking. What you see on their faces or in their eyes tells you instantly whether you are getting across. Such feedback is indispensable to being a professional speaker.

3. Always be audience-centric.

The truth is, in most cases, the attendees did not come to see or hear you speak. They came to learn something and feel differently, and laugh at loud, and cry, and think, and leave in better intellectual, attitudinal, spiritual, and emotional shape than they arrived. The quickest and most powerful way to connect with the audience is to learn the reason the organization exists and talk about it in terms of their published values and purpose, mentioning the names of their products and services, while giving a "shout out" to at least two or three key people in the audience who are superstars that epitomize your message.

This information is gathered during your mandatory "pre-conference call" with the meeting planner, which allows you to "customize" your remarks to their meeting theme and needs.

4. Make your presentation extremely personal.

There are two parts to every presentation: content and delivery. And... delivery always trumps content. You can be the world's foremost subject matter expert, but if you are a lousy speaker, lecturing instead of talking, killing your audience with power point slides instead of personally connecting with them using these Fifteen Platform/Performance Skills, your audience members will tune you out, while you confuse activity with accomplishment. Delivery also has two parts: verbal and non-verbal, with non-verbal always trumping verbal because the audience members always believe what they see.

It's true: "I'd rather see a sermon preached than hear one any day – I'd rather you would walk with me than merely point the way." Our posture and the way we dress and walk and act offstage and before our presentation matters more than what we say.

5. Tell your own stories.

In its simplest form, every speech/presentation has three parts: a beginning, middle, and an end – the introduction, the body, and the conclusion. The middle is a combination of "Social Proof" and "Researched Data Based Proof," where you tell your own stories to illustrate your points. This is the most important Skill on this list of fifteen and must always be formatted in the formula: make a point, tell a personal story to reinforce your point; make your next point; and reinforce it with another personal story. Your "Signature Story" is the most important story and should be shared in the first third of your speech/presentation, as it deepens your credibility and strengthens your connection to your listeners. This is because people don't relate to our perfections (if we even have any). They relate to our imperfections. They really don't care about our successes. They want to know if we have ever failed or fallen down and what we did to recover and get back up and go again.

Yes, some of our "Signature Stories" are about adventure and extraordinary accomplishment, but most involve overcoming obstacles, perseverance, and resiliency. And it is this extremely personal story that makes you unique, most believable, and a powerful example to every attendee that the best truly is yet to be!

WARNING: I was one of three keynote speakers for an all day event. Whenever possible, I attend the m

6. Ask questions.

The quickest way to get the attention of every audience member is to ask questions – especially in the first few seconds of your "Inside Introduction" and the five minutes that follow. Because you cannot - not answer a question, ask questions such as, "Do you believe..." followed by, "How many of you don't believe..." Raising your hand will get more to raise their hands.

7. Use humor.

Not an unrelated joke just for laughs, but a great line or short joke that not only breaks the ice, but has a message that helps you set up your "Thesis." If you are not naturally funny, this is where you use a hilarious slide or quick humorous video clip. Everybody loves to laugh as it triggers an increase in endorphins, and keeps the audience constantly tuned in for fear they will miss another chance to laugh again.

8. Make sure your stage moves have purpose.

Avoid body-swaying, weight-shifting, finger fidgeting, hair and clothing adjusting, and moving around too quickly and too much. When making your most significant points, always begin in the back half of center stage and move forward toward the audience. This psychologically hits home to your listeners that this point is critical.

9. Gestures and movement.

Use your hands to describe space and distance. If you are talking about something far away, in the future or visionary, extend your arm fully and point outward and upward if necessary. Use your hands to show the height and size of a person or thing. Use several fingers to count and keep the audience on track. Use an arm pump to accentuate and both arms up to signal touchdown, victory, oh yeah. Shrug your shoulders with your palms up to punctuate Who

162

knows? Who cares? and What's up? Use your body to illustrate and bring your characters to life. Use your imagination and let your inhibitions run wild in doing that which is necessary with your body to help your mouth paint the word pictures. And ... move! When you are on a large stage you must use the entire stage, talking to one group on one side for a few minutes, then to the other side of the stage for a few minutes. When you are going to make a most significant point it is critical that you make your way to center stage and walk to the front as you talk.

10. Just talk.

Don't lecture, exhort, expound, or try to baffle the audience with your bull sh*t multi-syllable vocabulary words. Talk with the same conversational inflections that you use in your home. Change the pitch of your voice. Give your listeners high pitches and low pitches full of unpredictable valleys and peaks. Change the volume of your voice. In every sentence you deliver there's at least one word that deserves selective emphasis. Yell, whisper, call out, quietly confide, reverently honor, and humbly plead—modulate your voice.

11. Enunciate clearly.

Focus your vocal pitch and volume on three representative people in each audience: the bored guy on the last row, the old man with the hearing aid in the middle of the room, and the foreign guest on the front row who doesn't understand English very well. Change the speed of your delivery. Talk clearly, loudly, and slowly enough that all three types of people just mentioned do not have to strain to hear you, understand you, be instructed, persuaded, and inspired.

12. Perfect the punctuating pause.

If you tell a story where the person dies at the end, pause and let him die. Let the audience feel the raw emotion before you move on. The same holds true with a joke. After you deliver the punch line, pause and let the audience laugh and enjoy themselves. Never start in too soon with more words. Let the listener wallow in the silence for an uncomfortable moment. Let the listener laugh until the laughter dies down. Only then should you proceed with your speech. No one likes to be cut off from enjoying the emotion of the moment. Stepping on the laughs or tears has the same emotional effect on us as having someone interrupt us just as we begin to sneeze a wonderful mighty sneeze!

13. Be animated.

Don't be afraid to pull faces, momentarily wear a prop, or go out in the audience to interact. The one eyebrow lift, the deer-in-the-headlights stare, the jaw drop "Oh my gosh," the blank stupid stare "I don't get it," and so forth. Don't be afraid to shock the audience by suddenly running across the stage or jumping up and down. For the dramatic effect, I personally kneel down on one knee at a key moment in every speech to get more intimate, up close, and personal with the listeners about a significant point I am making.

14. Direct the audience to get involved in your presentation.

This is not a license to use cheesy statements like, "Stand up and tell the person next to you that you love them." Personally, I treat my audiences with more sophisticated requests such as, "You are going to want to write this down." When appropriate you can actually have the audience engage in team teaching by asking the attendees to partner up and have one of them re-teach the other what you just taught the group.

15. Close with impeccability.

Just as their first impressions of you from your introduction must be congruent with your public persona that walks out onstage, so likewise must their last impressions be congruent with the speech your listeners just heard. As Max Dixon says, "Give your best expression, your best word choice to your close, and it will anchor a deep satisfaction between you and your audience." Give them an emotional amen, a quotable quote you personally wrote, and a memory of their experience with you that will echo in their minds, stir their souls, and be worthy of sharing long after the meeting adjourns.

EIGHT KEY COMMUNICATION TIPS FOR THE STAGE

- When finalizing what you are going to say in your speech, what is the one sentence that completely explains your message? Put your offering into one line. In case you run out of time, make sure you say what you came to say at the beginning!

- Paint a word picture of this most important point!

- When telling a story, cut out all the unnecessary information – delete the unnecessary details: kind of car, family members, etc. – cut right to the chase!

- If your audience members remember nothing else, what is the one thing – the single most important thing you want to leave with them? Yes, you need to tell the audience what you want them to remember – but never tell them to "write this down" – It makes you look like an amateur!

- When you tell a story, there is a difference between being "IN" the story, and as a narrator "OUT" of the story. Change positions on the stage from inside and outside the story – are you inside the story OR teaching the lessons learned from the story?

- All movement and gestures must have a purpose! Move across the stage for specific reasons. When you make the points of your speech, make first point on one side of the stage – make the second point two or three steps from where you started – make the next point a few steps from where you made the last point – and close at the other side of the stage. The most important points are always spoken front and center and louder.

- To help them know what the most important things are in your speech, speak faster during the rest of the presentation – and then slow down during the most important points and pause afterwards to let the audience process it before you move on.

- The difference between stage presentation talk and conversation talk is the use of "Conjunctions: but, and, um are not necessary or desired in a presentation. It's okay and preferred to just link one sentence into another.

CHAPTER EIGHTEEN

DO YOU FEEL WITH THE AUDIENCE?

People don't really care how much we know or what we have done. They only care about what they can learn from what we have learned. They want to be reminded that in life there are no mistakes, only lessons, that pain is a signal to grow, not to suffer. Consequently, people don't relate to our perfections; they relate to our imperfections. Most don't want to hear about our successes; they want to know if we ever failed or fell down and what we did to get back up and try again. If you think about it, when we turn on the news, we don't remember the facts and figures; we remember the interpretation of the facts and figures. We want to know how this information relates to us and our lives.

SATISFYING AUDIENCE NEEDS

In Maslow's hierarchy of human needs theory, Maslow suggests that certain needs take precedence over others. Physical needs are the most basic foundational needs because when neglected, they make responding to our other needs difficult. After we satisfy our physical needs, Maslow claims, Safety is critical, followed by feelings of be longing and that we are Loved. How these needs are satisfied before the meeting begins and how they are sustained throughout the presentation are both extremely important to the success of the speaker. Physical needs include food, shelter, touch, and water. Hungry people whose stomachs are growling don't concentrate well and really don't give a rat's-wa-kazoodle about building their positive self-esteem until they eat. Being thirsty isn't always a challenge before or during a meeting.

However, coffee and juices with breakfast and soft drinks during breaks are important, not only for energy and refreshment, but also because they affect the amount of time a meeting-goer can sit before taking a restroom break. Smokers need their breaks, and smoking a cigarette takes approximately eight minutes.

All of this suggests that the ideal break should be fifteen minutes long. Any longer allows the emotion and momentum you have created to diminish and weaken. The purpose of a break is to let the people take care of their *physical* needs, not check email or return calls. The most effective meetings are those that keep people focused on the theme, message, and purpose in a continuous emotional, intellectual way without distractions so that they experience something they cannot get at home or work.

When an audience is hungry or sitting too long, it is difficult to motivate them to follow your inspirational advice. They are motivated to stretch their legs, go to the snack shack, relieve their bladder, get a drink, or satisfy a real nicotine need. A "presenter" merely shows up and takes the microphone to whip off their "Speech A." A "professional speaker" communicates with the meeting planner ahead of time about where he will be on the program and what happens on the program before he is introduced. The true professional speaker suggests having a break right before he speaks if the audience has been sitting for more than sixty minutes.

In the meeting environment, the physical need for safety is obvious. However, to a professional speaker, safety is about creating a "Safe Environment," where the audience can openly talk about sensitive topics; where men don't feel weak or uncomfortable crying in public; where the audience can laugh and perhaps sing or jump or stand on our chairs and not feel stupid; and where they can feel safe to be real and in-the-moment, without inhibition.

In this vein, Safety meshes with Belonging and Love. Satisfying these needs is extremely important to a professional speaker. We all need to feel connected to others. We need affection, caring, inclusion, and relationships that make us feel like we fit in. This desire to be included and to be a part of something bigger than oneself is one of the most potent needs that a motivational speaker can utilize in reaching his audience.

Other approaches to fulfilling this need could include describing in your speech the admirable qualities you found in the group, such as the praiseworthy values, charitable natures, and other things that make them proud to be identified as part of the group.

The temperature of the room and the number of people that fit into the space of the room (crammed or roomy) also contribute to satisfying the audience's shelter needs. Trying to connect with and inspire a group that is sweltering from the heat or shivering with cold is an unnecessary and difficult burden to place on a speaker. When the seats are comfortable, the sound system is clear and at the appropriate volume, and the lighting evokes the ambience required for the theme, purpose, and message, then the motivational, persuasive professional speaker doesn't have to fight an uphill battle. He then has the perfect setting to turn attendees into listeners, make them feel loved and that they belong, and change their world one story at a time!

ROOM SET-UP AND CRITICAL MASS

As strange as it sounds, the way in which a room is set up directly influences the way the depth to which a speaker can connect with his audience. Chairs too far from the stage with the front row beginning out of the "intimate zone" or too many chairs and not enough people both disconnect the speaker from the audience. Because laughter and emotion are contagious, there is a critical mass necessary for a group to catch the fire of your speech.

Even in a very large room, if you can bunch the smaller group of people together, then you can get a powerful group effect that will help you reach the listeners. Having open seats between the audience members or vacant rows in front of them disrupts the fluid flow of emotion from stage to the convention floor and allows the laughter, tears, and inspirational message to weaken before it reaches each listener. Too much space between them will drain that energy away before the group effect can work at all.

Suggestion: Get to the room early for your sound check and use this time to suggest to the meeting planner that the back rows be taped or roped off like construction sites to make people move forward and fill up the room from front to back instead of the usual vice versa. If the room is set for five hundred and only one hundred fifty show up, they and your message are lost in that space. When more people come in late, it prevents you and your listeners from being disrupted as the latecomers fill in the back rows instead of the front rows. If all attendees come, take down the tape or rope and open the rear section.

On one occasion, when I was the second general session speaker at the Arkansas Bankers Association convention, I witnessed a clever way to better control meeting room space. I attended the first session so that I could tie in my remarks to the first presentation. The audience came early to get a back row seat, and the room quickly filled up, with every chair and row occupied from the rear forward, up to about the eighth row.

As the emcee concluded the introduction of the speaker from the empty front of the room, the speaker had his wireless microphone turned on, and immediately started talking in the back of the room. As the listeners cranked their heads around to see the speaker, he simply said, "Isn't it typical for all of us to sit in the back of our meetings so we can feel more casual and sleep or leave if the presenter is boring? Well, well, well. If I could ask each of you to turn your chairs around... this is now the new front of the room!

Brilliantly, this speaker took control of the situation and, as a true professional, didn't let any distractions alter the powerful impact he was committed to make!

CHAPTER NINETEEN

SHOULD YOU SELL FROM THE STAGE?

There are Five Reasons people don't buy: No Money, No Time, No Need, No Urgency, No Trust. Everything falls under these categories. It's never about the money; it's never about price. We've all purchased something that costs a little more from someone we trust. It's never about time. Show me the value and I'll make the time! Tell me I Need it and that's not enough. The key is to establish Urgency.

When we want to sell from stage, our primary job is to create a sense of Urgency! Attendees/Prospects are so focused on price that they don't realize how bad they need it!

Overcoming Meeting Planner Objections

What if the meeting planner does not pre-purchase, order your book, or allow you to host a signing or mention your products from the platform? What works for me is to have a copy of my book at the podium and, during the course of my speech, ask at least two evocative questions, and then pause while I quickly look up the answers in my book. Reading a powerful quote, sharing specific statistics, or relating a poem or song lyric that they can't get any other place sparks the attendees' curiosity to want to get their hands on the source of this unique information. It's also valuable to include something like, "I don't have time to cover all twelve concepts that are included in my book, so let me just share four." Then read the four steps straight from the book, and casually close it, and discuss. This technique creates curiosity and gets people to buy your book during or after your speech, and gets them to trust you when you get to the point of your speech when you sell from stage.

TWO PROVEN PRODUCT-SELLING SUGGESTIONS

1. Pre-sell. When the meeting planner books you on the program, suggest they purchase your book for each attendee. The following dialogue has successfully worked for my office: "I am thrilled to see that you have secured Dan for your June 16 meeting, and look forward to working with you on this event. I'd like to send you a proposal with a copy of each of Dan's books for you to review and decide if you're interested in gifting one or more to your audience members. I'm sure anyone attending Dan's session would be delighted with such a great take-away gift. Each time a story or principle is read or shared, Dan's messages of empowerment, productivity, and positive attitude will be brought home again and again—a pretty powerful motivational tool that will keep Dan's philosophy on passionate living current long after his keynote speech has ended." If the meeting planners simply do not want to or don't have the budget to pre-buy, then offer to host a book signing after your presentation, at no cost to the client, where the audience members can choose to buy your products after your presentation.

2. To sell from the platform with confidence, you must honestly believe you are providing a vital resource and will be giving the audience an unfinished program unless they take home your book (as if they are leaving an award-winning three-act play at the end of the second act!). We speakers are there to make a difference. It's true that most attendees didn't come expecting to buy. They assumed they would just sit there and— *abracadabra!*—magically change. But if the speaker doesn't give them everything he knows to help them take it to the next level, the speaker is doing a disservice. Our products are there to

reinforce and expand on what we can cover in the brief time we spend on the platform.

So that the attendees don't feel "sold to" (which translates into them being offended and not responding to back-of-the-room sales), we need only couch our resource pitch as the way to have us there with them at work and home to support them as they try to change. It's about providing practical and applicable value beyond your hour together and the content of your speech.

BEST SALES AND MARKETING CLOSE

Immediately before you go into the powerful conclusion to your speech, the following offer should be made: "Before I close, let me express my thanks to each of you for being here and extend a sincere plea that if there is anything else I can do to help you make the changes you seek in your life, meet me in the back of the room when this session is over and I'll share some additional ways I can be of service." If you don't have books or handouts, this is where you provide order forms and contact information, reminding them that the package they can get through your office is the total program solution to what they experienced with you that day. With this "I must maintain contact" seed now planted in their minds and hearts, go into your planned, practiced speech conclusion remembering what I've cited before, "Reason leads to conclusions, but it is emotion that leads to action!"

CHAPTER TWENTY

WILL YOU CUSTOMIZE EVERY PRESENTATION?

Now that you understand the science of regurgitating and recalling your own powerful 'Significant Emotional Events' and uncovering the life lessons you learned from each of them; and because you have also chosen which of these experiences is your 'Signature Story' that defines who you are and delivers your 'Last Lecture' message to the world; and because you now have written out your stories to know their length and have replaced the ordinary verbs with an assortment of extraordinary active/word picture verbs, you are ready to learn how to 'customize' each speech.

Once you have been asked to speak to a certain group on a specific date and have confirmed the engagement with a signed contract (even when you are donating your time and talents with no remuneration for services), it is critical that you require a 'Conference Phone Call' with the meeting planner and/or committee, to discuss all the details. It is during this mandatory pre-meeting call when you ask the meeting planner(s) the twelve questions and subsequent follow up inquiries that let you 'customize' your speech.

TWELVE KEY CUSTOMIZING QUESTIONS

Theme?

1. **Does this meeting have a specific published Theme?** – How did you come up with it? What does it mean to you? What was your Theme last year, why, and how does it tie into this year's theme? Who spoke in my slot last year and what was his/her message?

Purpose?

2. **What is the Purpose of this meeting?** – Is it an annual event? Is it mandatory or voluntary attendance? What is the history of this event – how long have you held it? Is its primary purpose networking (a customer event), education (to receive CEU credits), motivation, training?

Attendees?

3. **Who are the Attendees?** – How many people will be attending? What are their specific job titles, descriptions and responsibilities? What do they specifically do when they come to work? If they are sales professionals, whom do they call on? Are they on 100% commission or base plus commission/bonuses? What is the average income of the attendees?

Primary Products/Services?

4. **What are the Primary Products and Services you provide/sell?** What is the specific name, feature, and benefit of your strongest selling product/service? What does it do? What is the name, feature, and benefit of your weakest selling product/service? What does it do? Why does it not sell and what do you think would increase sales?

Your Desired Message?

5. **What is your desired Message?** – If you were speaking in my slot on the program, what would you say? What are the three most important things to you that I can echo in my speech to validate what you have been teaching and advocating? Are there any sensitive issues you need me to avoid? Do you have any specific organizational "buzz" words or marketing/sales slogans that are part of your branding and popular with your group that

I can amalgamate into my speech? What is your bottom line "call to action" and desired ROI when the meeting concludes?

Public Acknowledgements?

6. Whom should I acknowledge and Publicly Thank in the audience? Which person or committee/team deserves peer recognition for his/her leadership and involvement in the meeting? What are the names and job descriptions, and explain why you feel this way?

   The beauty in this telephone exchange with the customer is that as you are asking the questions, and they are answering and unveiling their specific meeting needs. You are writing down the names of your stories, analogies, anecdotes, and quotes that you will incorporate into your speech, which gives them ownership of your message and literally engages them in helping you write your speech!

Year To Date Organizational Performance?

7. How has your Organizational Performance been this year? Have you met your numbers? If so, why? If not, why not? What is the general attitude and moral of the attendees? What is the best part of their job? What is the most challenging part of their job?

Organizational Culture?

8. Will you please describe your Organizational Culture? Send me a copy of your Vision, Purpose, and Mission Statements, and a list of your Core Values, so I can inculcate them into my presentation. (If they are going through a merger/acquisition it is critical to know this so you can incorporate a team building/"one mind – one heart – one purpose" message into your remarks.)

Two Superstars?

9. May I Interview Two Super-Successful People who will be at the meeting, to find out what they are thinking and doing that makes them extraordinary? (When possible and feasible.) May I visit one of your offices/stores/locations to see what you do and how you do it, and talk to the leader, officer, manager, superintendent, to get his/her take on what they think I should address in my upcoming speech that will assist them to do their jobs?

Position On Program?

10. What is my Position on your program? Is it an opening general session kickoff keynote speaker to set the tone for the entire meeting? Or a closing general session capstone speaker to tie a bow around the entire meeting, and leave them on a high to leave and immediately implement what they have learned to strengthen their personal relationships, improve professional performance? What happens before my speech? Breakout workshop sessions? Other speakers? Award presentation? What happens after my speech?

Meeting Start Time?

11. What is the Meeting Start Time so as to schedule the AV Sound Check? When do the attendees begin to enter the room? Will you please have the audio/visual technician and the person in charge of managing the program meet me in the meeting room one hour before the actual meeting begins?

My Start Time?

12. What is My Specific Start Time? How long do you want me to speak?

CHAPTER TWENTY-ONE

WILL YOU GIVE AN AMAZING MEDIA INTERVIEW?

You already know the most important part of the answer. First, you must know what you believe. To get a better answer, you must ask a better question. Ask yourself the easy and especially the tough questions and respond to them honestly and completely. You can fool others for a while, but you can never fool yourself. Therefore, always tell the truth. If and when you tell the truth, you don't have to worry about remembering anything!

Back in the stage of figuring out what you would drive five hours to say to someone for free, you were invited to decide what your personal message is. And if your experiences, discovered meaning, and practical purpose in life invoke a deep conviction that public speaking is a 'calling,' then responding to someone's questions on or off camera, onstage or offstage, on-air or off-air, or on the record or off the record is no big deal.

You know what you know; people want to know it and learn from you and, through a question-and-answer process, you tell them. Once you know what your message is, research the topic thoroughly and memorize key facts, quotes from experts, and chapter and verse sources of time-tested data that you can repeat at any time during any interview. The critical point here is that you understand the difference between an interview with you posed as an expert eyewitness 'reporter' and you just sharing your 'opinion.' Either way, you need to know what you're talking about and come across as someone who has spent a great deal of time thinking about this subject.

FIVE SIMPLE STEPS TO GIVING AN AMAZING MEDIA INTERVIEW

Among the five suggestions, the first two are the most important:

1. Keep every answer to thirty seconds.

This is so the interviewer has time to ask you as many questions as possible in the time allocated. This makes the interview flow and keeps it much more interesting. Thirty-second answers must be practiced and rehearsed. As you ask yourself the easy and the toughest questions and give yourself, and perhaps a friend or coach, the long complete answer, continue to practice this process until, through an intense editing process, you finally end up with your concise but conversational thirty-second reply.

2. Take charge.

Before the interview begins, decide what specific messages, points of interest, facts, and short stories you need to share. Decide on the specific image you need to convey and what nonverbal elements must be used to be judged as you need to be judged, such as hairstyle and length; business or business casual attire; color of shirt, suit, and tie.

Oftentimes you are told the interview will last ten minutes, and when you arrive, they have reduced your time to three minutes. When you already know the most important thing you want to bring up and get out of the interview, this diminishing of your opportunity doesn't stress you out. You simply edit your thoughts and make sure you get to your point immediately. This 'getting to your point' and 'taking charge of every interview' is different than taking control. The one asking the questions is always in control of the conversation. However, taking charge is knowing what you want to talk about. Therefore, regardless of the question asked, you can turn it into an opportunity to get your point across. In the world of great interview skills it's known as "bridging."

When the interviewer throws you a curve question that you either don't want to answer or don't have time to answer if you are to keep to your agenda, the three simplest "bridges" are:

- "Before I get to that, let me fill you in…"
- "Let us consider the larger issue here…"
- "Instead of that, you should ask me about…"
- "Let me tell you what happened…"

Bridging can get you out of the most difficult situations. Example: OJ Simpson went on trial for the murders of his wife, Nicole, and Ron Goldman. The televised trial started on the first day of camp of the next NFL football season. Reporters were everywhere. I was at the Raiders camp in Oxnard, California, and not one question relevant to football was asked to any player. All the television reporters wanted to know about their personal lives. Microphones were literally stuck in the faces of every prominent athlete with personal inquiries: 'How many times have you beat your girlfriend?' 'Have you ever abused your wife?' 'Did you have an abusive father and come from a dysfunctional family situation?'

Rather than answer these questions, and instead of avoiding the media altogether, a player could have replied with his own platform message, "The real question here is can we leave our work at the office and balance out our lives? All of us men need to make sure our personal relationships with our wives and family are good and positive. And in order to do this, we must realize that before we can respect someone else, we must first respect ourselves. This is the secret to building a winning family and a winning team, which is the only reason I am at football camp. Like my teammates, I want to get better every day so that, together, we can win the championship this year!'

When Alexander the Great invaded India, he brought before him wise men and asked them a question. To spice things up, he said if they got the answer wrong they would be put to death. Question: 'Which is the most cunning of beasts?' The answer they gave, which saved their lives: 'That which man has not discovered.' Brilliant, eh? The wise men lived.

Bridging gets you from where you are in the conversation to where you would rather be. The best guests don't evade the difficult questions. If you ignore them, they will be asked again. In this case, restructure the question before answering by offering additional information not required by the question. If you were asked if you supported President Bush's policy in Iraq, which is extremely controversial and will immediately divide your listeners into pro and con mode, you would restructure the question:

That is a fascinating question. I think all of us need to ask ourselves about this concept of support.'

When we say we support the troops, we must ask ourselves what we are supporting. Could we support the troops and not Bush? Did you support the fact that President Bush has appointed more women and more minorities and has given more money for AIDS research and African AIDS relief than any other U.S. president in history? Do you support your Senator, who voted yes on this issue and yet no on these major bills?" Give reliable facts and credible statistics in your new information and they will never come back to the original, difficult, controversial question!

To minimize the hazards of being interviewed, remember three things: be prepared, have conviction, and express your facts and opinions with enthusiasm! If you are not excited about your message, why should anyone else be? Be anecdotal. Use examples and quick, short, powerful stories that the audience will remember.

3. Wardrobe.

You are the message, not your clothing. Never wear anything so odd, controversial, or flashy that it draws attention away from you to your outfit.

For men, avoid white shirts and light blue everything. Gray, darker blues, yellows, and beige are best for the camera. Black is to be avoided because it absorbs too much light. Wear knee-high socks that are darker than your pants so that you never show bare calf. Always wear a solid-colored shirt and a solid-colored suit or sports jacket. Only one thing can be patterned and that is your tie. Men should never get more casual than a sports jacket in lieu of a suit. Expensive-looking designer sweaters will work if the specific show and demographic of the viewer calls for it.

These rules also apply to women. Find out what color the backdrop is so your clothing does not clash. You are always safe with the neutral colors of brown, khaki, navy, and gray. Use your judgment and the opinion of at least one other person as to whether your top is see-through and whether your skirt or dress is the appropriate length. Try your wardrobe out while sitting and have someone tell you what message you look like you are trying to send. Remember, bright lights on dark cloth seem to penetrate and reveal the underwear underneath.

Be careful of stripes (especially horizontal) and plaids, because a television camera makes you appear about ten pounds heavier. Avoid prints with flowers, animals, busy geometric circles or squares, and showing too much leg, or the viewers will watch the dress or body instead of listening to you.

4. Vocabulary and humor.

We all know flamboyant people who not only use big words in their conversation, but just plain talk too much. In fact, we never have to worry about these people "passing gas" or "cutting cheese" because they don't shut up long enough to build up the required pressure! Although the host interviewing you may have done some research and checked out your website to become familiar with you and your message, it does not follow that the TV viewers or radio listeners have prepared themselves to tune into the program.

They don't know the unique and special jargon of your profession or the intricacies of your organization so don't talk over their heads. Why call it "attitudinal conditioning" when you can just say "positive thinking"? Or why talk about "maldistribution of primary health care deliverers" when you can simply refer to it as a "shortage of family doctors in the country"? Military officers and NCOs are guilty of excluding non-military listeners when they talk in their infamous acronyms: "This TQM is important over in the AOR so our troops RWH."

Part of vocabulary is a sense of humor. I'm not talking about telling jokes here. I'm talking about what I call "practiced spontaneity." Long before the speech is delivered, you come up with hilarious comebacks for when something unexpected happens. If someone sneezes loudly, you immediately say, "Bless you, and that's exactly what I'm talking about. If you're going to sneeze, sneeze to the very best of your ability." Hire a humor writer to help you come up with something intimately funny about each state and each capitol city. There are only fifty of each and you should memorize your funny comments so you can interact with the audience and have something to say to every person, no matter where they are from.

This holds true with a TV or radio interview. If you have a memorized quote and answer always on the tip of your tongue, ready to use in a conversational manner in response to an interviewer's question, you come across to the viewers and listeners as one of the brightest and funniest people who ever lived. The rule with humor is that if it does not come naturally to you, don't force it—don't use it.

However, if being funny is being you, then don't shut it off when the camera or studio red light turns on. Use it and milk it in a natural way. If you're going to be plugging your book on a political talk show, memorize and practice your "spontaneity" with some quick, political one-liners. If it's a sports or educational program, make sure your repertoire includes funny comments about your interview topic and your viewing or listening audience.

5. Mind-set.

When you are being interviewed on television or radio, think of yourself as an invited guest in someone's living room, politely waiting to give your opinion or factual expertise on a subject. Talk to the host or other guests in the same conversational way you would without the cameras, lights, and microphones around. If you can, imagine the camera as a person and talk directly to it whenever you make a significant point inclusive to your predetermined, specific message.

Remember, your listeners and viewers are watching you through the camera lens, and if you can glance at that lens as you would glance across a room, making eye contact with everyone present, you'll come across well. If you suddenly get a frog in your throat or an intense need to cough, don't fight it. Take care of it immediately. It happens to everybody and this demonstrates your "realness," approachability, and humanity. Simply turn away from the microphone, whether on television or radio, and cough or clear your throat. Making a "farm animal noise" is far better than choking to death and causing a real scene!

Plant yourself firmly in the chair. Sit erect so you don't create rolls around your waist and leaves your chest cavity uncompressed so you can speak without running out of breath. Never cross your arms, but it is good to cross your legs or ankles as it gives you a more relaxed and confident look.

CHAPTER TWENTY-TWO

WHY EVENT/MEETING PLANNERS WILL HIRE YOU

"8 BUYING TRIGGERS"

When evaluating and choosing their next speaker, event/ meeting planners will put you at the top of their list because you have explained the eight things every event/meeting professional wants to know:

1. How Can You Specifically Serve My Organization?
2. What Specific Problems Will You Solve?
3. You Are An Expert Who Speaks – Explain Your Topics And Messages.
4. What Are Your 'Credibility Boosters'?
5. How Are You Staying Current – Why Is Your Message Relevant?
6. You Are Easy To Work With– Examples Of Being Accommodating.
7. You Have Real World Experience – Interviews And Adventures To Share
8. You Are Authentic – Were Ordinary Before You Became Extraordinary.

Create a "One Sheet" – title it:

The Top Seven Reasons You Should Hire (your name) _____
(EXAMPLE)

1. While you are asking your questions during your preconference telephone call you, are writing down the titles of the stories you choose to tell, and jotting down keywords that will allow you to customize your material and research data to meet the needs of the event/meeting planner. This allows you to answer the first two questions on the mind of every event/meeting planner: how you will serve the organization, and what problems will you solve.

2. Dan is an expert in Motivation/Resiliency, Leadership, Team Building, Story Selling and Change. Dan's keynote speeches and training/coaching programs make:

   - Self Mastery Permanent
   - Winning Personal
   - Leadership Automatic

Motivation/Resiliency

Dan played American football for 13 years. Was paralyzed for fourteen months. Went to sixteen doctors. Fifteen said he would not recover. By following the steps of resilience he did.

Leadership

Dan is the CEO and founder of a multi-million-dollar international communications firm and Character and Leadership Development Consultant for the United States Military.

Team Building

Dan has turned around struggling companies and has worked with many of the teams in the National Football League where he has transformed last place NFL teams into Super Bowl Champions.

Story-Selling

As a master storyteller, Dan has been published in more than 50 million books in 50 languages worldwide. Dan is also a Gold Record Songwriter who knows how to "edit so every word pays its own way!" Dan is a student of how Brain Chemicals affect our decision-making and teaches how speakers/leaders/sales professionals can choose the necessary story to trigger a specific chemical to influence results in every situation.

3. Dan was sponsored by internationally recognized and beloved Zig Ziglar into the world of professional speaking in 1982, who for 30 years mentored Dan in the art and science of motivational teaching. In 1987, Dan earned the prestigious CSP – Certified Speaking Professional designation bestowed by the National Speakers Association. In 1999, Dan was named one of the Top Ten Speakers In The World by Achievers Global. In 2005, Dan was inducted into the National Speakers Hall of Fame. In 2015, Dan was again named one of the Top Ten Motivational Speakers In The World by sSpeakers, and continues to be one of the most in-demand speakers on the planet!

Since 1982, Dan has spoken to more than 6 million people, in over 5500 audiences, in all 50 states, in 75 countries, on 6 continents to most of the Fortune 500, to NASA, Super Bowl Champions, Million Dollar Round Table and multiple times to our combat troops on the front lines in Iraq, Afghanistan, Asia and Africa.

4. As the modern-day Napoleon Hill Dan remains relevant with Millenials, GenExers, and Baby Boomers because he continuously interviews the world's most successful and fascinating people, while seeking the next extreme adventure to learn life's greatest lessons from those who know what works, what doesn't and why. Dan has soared to the edge of space in a U2 Spy Plane where he witnessed the curvature of the earth, has flown with the Air Force Thunderbirds, raced automobiles at Nürburgring, and served on the Olympic Committee and carried the Olympic Torch in the 2002 Winter Games.

5. Dan has NEVER missed a speech. Dan's office staff always keeps you posted on every aspect of Dan's travels, notifies you when he arrives and checks in, and if flights cancel, Dan rents a car! Dan's office staff takes pride in both speed and efficiency in sending out the 'Speaker Packet,' returning contracts, sending Dan's Media Kit and answering every question on a daily basis. Dan's reputation is 'low maintenance, fun loving, self deprecating, accommodating.

6. Dan has "Real Life/Real World Experience" so he speaks as an eyewitness, as one having authority. Highlights of Dan's resume' include playing on and coaching championship teams, serving as a Leadership and Character Development Consultant for the United States military, acquiring immense knowledge and wisdom to formulate cutting edge proven processes and time-tested solutions that he has published in 37 bestselling books, and most significant, Dan was named Utah Father of the Year in 2012!

7. Dan serves on the International Board of Governors of Operation Smile – a humanitarian organization of volunteer physicians, nurses, dentists and medical practitioners who perform free reconstructive facial surgery on children in developing countries

who were tragically born with a cleft lip/ cleft pallet. Dan's heart is big and his philanthropic generosity is far reaching, which keeps him humble, charismatic, fascinating, engaging, inspirational, authentic, and the same off stage as he is on stage. Dan loves to interact with your people at every level, and is eager to do book signings, meet and greets and attend your reception the night before he speaks!

"OPPORTUNITIES AND SPEAKER'S HONORARIUM"

According to Mike Frank, past president of the National Speakers Association and owner of Speakers Unlimited – there are 100 major bureaus in North America, who average 500 bookings per year, which means 50,000 paid speaking engagements are contracted every year by bureaus and hundreds more directly with speakers⬚

According to "Smart Meetings Magazine," which meeting planners and conference producers contribute to and read, there are Five Levels of Speakers Honorariums. In an answer to the question, "Should I charge what the prospective client's budget is?" The answer is an emphatic No! Know your worth! Believe you have been 'Called' to change people's lives! Let your fellow Subject Matter Experts in your field set your speaker's fee!

FIVE LEVELS

1. If you are an Unpaid Speaker: perceived as just starting out.

2. $1000 to $2500: You are perceived as an amateur "wanna be" and they know 'you get what you pay for!'

3. $2500 to $5000: You are someone who is transitioning from part-time – you are still a dabbler – still not really a professional speaker – still earning your 'wings⬚'

4. $5,000 to $10,000: You are looked at as a serious expert and they are hiring a true professional!"

5. $10,000 to $20,000 and above: You are a celebrity, New York Times Best Selling Author, or a marquee name.

REMEMBER:

The purpose of a meeting is to take the attendees on an unforgettable roller coaster ride to an intellectual and emotional place they can't take themselves, and give them an experience they can't get at home or work, so they leave your speech saying, 'I like me best when I'm with you, I want to see you again.'

CHAPTER TWENTY-THREE

THE REVIEW

18 POINTS OF THE ART AND SCIENCE OF SIGNIFICANT PUBLIC SPEAKING

1. **What are the three questions and accompanying titles revealed in the Speakers Triangle that every listener needs the answers to?**

    1. Why Should I Listen To You? Historical/Current. "Credibility."
    2. Can I Do It Too? With my weaknesses/Limitations/Strengths. "Possibility."
    3. What Do I Do Next? How Do I Get From Where I Am To Where I Want To Be? "Usability."

2. **What are the titles and one-line descriptions of the "Six Steps to Crafting a Speech Listener's Love"?**

    Shhh!

    In The Intro: Get attention – Shush, listen to this – this speaker will be amazing.
    In The Speech: the first 30 to 60 seconds is most important – get everybody's attention.

    Huh?

    Okay, you've got my attention, now keep it. Smiling and eye contact are crucial.

Why?

Why did you bring this up? The next 2 to 5 minutes of your speech where you start to "stretch" my mind. Build a bridge from the stage to the audience. Make it relevant to me.

How?

Give me proof. Intensify the "stretch" connecting the head with the heart. Tell me the stories. Quote me credible statistics. Inspire me – make me laugh, think and feel.

Where?

Where do I go from here? One speech can't change me – what other resources, books and recorded material do you recommend to keep the "stretch" alive? Where is "The System?"

When?

When should I take action on what you spoke about? The "Emotional Close." Leave them wanting more.

3. **What are the "Eight Elements of Organizing a Powerful Presentation"?**

- Outside Introduction – written by you to be read by another to establish your credibility. (Tied into the first step "Shhh" in the Six Steps To Crafting A Speech Listener's Love)

- Inside Introduction – the first 30 to 60 seconds of your speech, followed by the next two to five minutes that build on the first. (Tied into the second and third steps "Huh" and "Why?" in the Six Steps To Crafting A Speech Listener's Love)

- Thesis – the stated purpose for your speech/presentation. (Tied into the third step "Why" in the Six Steps To Crafting A Speech Listener's Love)

- Structure – the score-keeping template that organizes your remarks. (Tied into the fourth step "How" in the Six Steps To Crafting A Speech Listener's Love)

- Social Proof – the stories and illustrations in the body of your speech/presentation. (Tied into the fourth step "How" in the Six Steps To Crafting A Speech Listener's Love)

- Researched Data Based Proof – the reliable and quoted sources that back up your Thesis. (Tied into the fourth step "How" in the Six Steps To Crafting A Speech Listener's Love)

- Visual Aid Support – the PowerPoint slides/video that conceptualize and make visual your researched data. (Tied into the fourth step "How" in the Six Steps To Crafting A Speech Listener's Love)

- Conclusion / Call To Action – the emotional conclusion to your speech/ presentation. (Tied into the fifth and sixth steps "Where" "When" in the Six Steps To Crafting A Speech Listener's Love)

4. **Is the Introduction part of the speech?**

Yes.

5. **Should you write your own Introduction, or send your bio to the meeting planner and let him/her write what they think is interesting and important?**

Write your own Introduction – which is the Outside Introduction.

6. What is the optimum length of an Outside Introduction?

Two and a half minutes.

7. What is the optimum length of your Inside Introduction?

Two to five minutes.

8. What is FEAR?

F.E.A.R. does not mean: Forget Everything And Run. FEAR is: False Evidence Appearing Real – which means you always: Face EverythingAnd Rise, because courage is being scared to death and saddling up anyway!

9. What are the four ways you can overcome nervousness?

- Always see your audience as recipients, not critics.
- Prepare, memorize, and practice exactly how you will begin and end your speech/presentation.
- Practice every one of your illustrative stories until you can tell them without notes.
- Accept every speaking opportunity so you can practice and practice.

10. What is Plagiarism?

Anytime you present another person's work as your own, even if that other person is a friend and/or spouse, you have plagiarized. "Plagiarism is the act of appropriating any other person's or group's ideas or work (written, computerized, artistic, etc.) or portions thereof and passing them off as the product of one's own work in any academic exercise or activity."

11. What is an Ethical Speaker?

A speaker who never lies.

12. Although no speech is purely one mode, what are the Five Delivery Modes in public speaking?

- Impromptu – off the cuff
- Extemporaneous – delivered from notes
- Manuscript – written out and read
- Memorized – delivered word for word
- Conversational – written out so you can time it / then practiced so many times that you move from "word-bound memorization" to a natural style with the same eye contact, gestures, smile, body language and voice inflections that you would have if you were sitting at a restaurant having dinner with a friend.

13. What are the Seven Speech Categories?

- Entertaining Speech: Usually a luncheon or after dinner speech with a light message, lots of laughs, under 30 minutes long!

- Persuasive Speech: A persuasive speech specifically focuses on your ability to craft a coherent argument about a topic that is both relevant and interesting in *your* life, which makes us believe and agree with you so we engage in your cause!

- Informative Speech: Focused on your ability to teach and inform your listener(s) about a topic both interesting and relevant in *their* lives.

- Instructor Speech: Specific Training through a hands-on experience to teach a new and specialized new skill set.

- Impromptu Speech: No, they are not "off-the-cuff" as most believe, but rather, "spur-of-the-moment" opportunities to express ourselves in an organized delivery using the "Eight Elements of Organizing a Speech."

- Extemporaneous Speech: Either persuasive or informative in nature, with little or no advance preparation, which validates that you should spend less time preparing a speech and more time preparing yourself to speak.

- Three Different Special Occasion Speeches: A Tribute, a Toast, and a Eulogy.

14. What are the two parts of "Practiced Spontaneity?"

- Itemizing what unexpected things could happen during your speech and memorizing a humorous response to each – sneeze, excessive coughing, lights go out, microphone stops working, etc.

- Itemize capital cities, facts about different social, political, racial groups, and memorize humorous comments about each one.

15. What are the Four Purposes of a Speech?

- To Entertain
- To Persuade
- To Inform
- To Teach

16. What are the Four Visual Aid Support Options?

- Photos/Slides
- Flow Charts
- Graphs
- Video Clips

17. What are the three most common Speech Organizers in a "Structured" speech?

- Sign Posts (a reminder of how far you've come and how far you have to go)
- Numbering (organizing key points into 1,2,3,4)
- Acronyms (forming a new word from the first letter of a series of words)

18. What are the Four Reasons why you require a "Sound Check" one hour before anyone enters the room where you will be speaking?

- To check room set up and walk the stage, determine where to enter and exit the stage, check out the set (plants, obstacles) and to see the lighting scheme and podium positioning.
- To check your microphone request – at the podium, clip-on lavaliere or handheld wireless.
- To check if your requested CD, DVD player, laptop, projector and screen are hooked up with an operator to run them.
- To meet the person who is going to introduce you so you can personally hand him/her your Intro and ask him/her to read it verbatim.

OTHER BOOKS AVAILABLE
BY DAN CLARK

- The Art of Significance-Achieving The Level Beyond Success (Audiobook Also Available)
- The Art of Significance Study Guide Training Manual
- The Art of Significant Relationships
- The Art of Raising Significant Children
- Influential Impact – The Art of Significant Leadership
- Transference of Trust – The Art of Significant Selling
- Making of a Champion – The Art of Significant Team Building
- The Art of Significant Network Marketing
- (Audiobook and Study Guide)
- Speak Like A Pro – The Art and Science of Significant Public Speaking
- Story Selling – How to Persuade People to Think, Feel, Act, Follow, Buy
- Chicken Soup for the College Soul
- The Most Popular Stories By Dan Clark In Chicken Soup For The Soul
- Puppies for Sale (Illustrated Children's Storybook)
- Soul Food (The Complete Dan Clark Story Collection)
- Dan Clark's Humor File – A Repository of Jokes and B.S. Tales
- The Treasury of Dan Clark Quotes, Lyrics and Poems

www.ingramcontent.com/pod-product-compliance
Lightning Source LLC
Chambersburg PA
CBHW031932190326
41519CB00007B/502